Company's Coming ®
Greatest Hits

Sandwiches & Wraps

www.**companys**coming.com
visit our web-site

Over 175 best-selling recipes

GREATEST HITS SERIES

Sandwiches & Wraps

First printing April 2000

Canadian Cataloguing in Publication Data
Paré, Jean
   Greatest hits: sandwiches & wraps

Issued also in French under title: Jean Paré grands
succès : sandwiches et roulés.
(Greatest hits series)
Includes index.
ISBN 1-896891-37-3

   1. Sandwiches. I. Title. II. Title: Sandwiches &
wraps. III. Series.

TX818.P37 2000   641.8'4   C00-900049-6

Published simultaneously in Canada
and the United States of America by
The Recipe Factory Inc. in conjunction with
Company's Coming Publishing Limited
2311 - 96 Street, Edmonton, Alberta,
Canada T6N 1G3
Tel: 780 • 450-6223
Fax: 780 • 450-1857
www.companyscoming.com

Company's Coming is a registered trademark owned
by Company's Coming Publishing Limited
Printed in Canada

FRONT COVER:

1. Chicken Curry Filling, page 62
2. Cream Cheese And Grape Jelly
   Sandwich, page 76
3. Salad Envelopes, page 112
4. Fruity Chicken Pitas, page 92
5. Muffuletta, page 96
6. Pepper Cheese Roll, page 25
7. Dill Pickle Sandwich, page 76

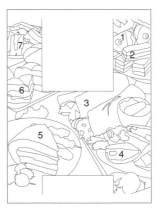

Props Courtesy Of: Stokes
                        X/S Wares

www.companyscoming.com
visit our web-site

table of contents

our cookbooks

COMPANY'S COMING SERIES

150 Delicious Squares
Appetizers
Breads
Breakfasts & Brunches
Cakes
Casseroles
Chicken, Etc.
Cookies
Cooking for Two
Desserts
Dinners of the World
Fish & Seafood
Holiday Entertaining
Kids Cooking
Light Casseroles
Light Recipes
Lunches
Main Courses
Meatless Cooking
Microwave Cooking
Muffins & More
One-Dish Meals
Pasta
Pies
Pizza!
Preserves
Salads
Slow Cooker Recipes
Soups & Sandwiches
Starters
Stir-Fry - **NEW**
Vegetables

ASSORTED TITLES

Beef Today!
Easy Entertaining
Kids Lunches

GREATEST HITS

Biscuits, Muffins & Loaves
Dips, Spreads & Dressings
Soups & Salads - **NEW**
Sandwiches & Wraps - **NEW**

LIFESTYLE SERIES

Grilling - **NEW**
Low-fat Cooking
Low-fat Pasta

SELECT SERIES

30-Minute Meals
Beans & Rice
Ground Beef
Make-Ahead Salads
No-Bake Desserts
Sauces & Marinades

company's coming story

ean Paré grew up understanding that the combination of family, friends and home cooking is the essence of a good life. From her mother she learned to appreciate good cooking, while her father praised even her earliest attempts. When she left home she took with her many acquired family recipes, a love of cooking and an intriguing desire to read recipe books like novels!

In 1963, when her four children had all reached school age, Jean volunteered to cater the 50th anniversary of the Vermilion School of Agriculture, now Lakeland College. Working out of her home, Jean prepared a dinner for over 1000 people which launched a flourishing catering operation that continued for over eighteen years. During that time she was provided with countless opportunities to test new ideas with immediate feedback—resulting in empty plates and contented customers! Whether preparing cocktail sandwiches for a house party or serving a hot meal for 1500 people, Jean Paré earned a reputation for good food, courteous service and reasonable prices.

"Why don't you write a cookbook?" Time and again, as requests for her recipes mounted, Jean was asked that question. Jean's response was to team up with her son, Grant Lovig, in the fall of 1980 to form Company's Coming Publishing Limited. April 14, 1981, marked the debut of "150 DELICIOUS SQUARES", the first Company's Coming cookbook in what soon would become Canada's most popular cookbook series.

Jean Paré's operation has grown steadily from the early days of working out of a spare bedroom in her home. Full-time staff includes marketing personnel located in major cities across Canada. Home Office is based in Edmonton, Alberta in a modern building constructed specially for the company.

Today the company distributes throughout Canada and the United States in addition to numerous overseas markets, all under the guidance of Jean's daughter, Gail Lovig. Best-sellers many times over, Company's Coming cookbooks are published in English and French, plus a Spanish-language edition is available in Mexico. Familiar and trusted in home kitchens the world over, Company's Coming cookbooks are offered in a variety of formats, including the original softcover series.

Jean Paré's approach to cooking has always called for quick and easy recipes using everyday ingredients. Even when traveling, she is constantly on the lookout for new ideas to share with her readers. At home, she can usually be found researching and writing recipes, or working in the company's test kitchen. Jean continues to gain new supporters by adhering to what she calls "the golden rule of cooking": never share a recipe you wouldn't use yourself. It's an approach that works—*millions of times over!*

foreword

The sandwich has been with us since the late 1700s and was named after its creator, John Montagu, the 4th Earl of Sandwich. It was his habit to "sandwich" his meat between thick slices of bread. Since then, creating combinations of filling and ways to enclose them has been an ongoing challenge in our kitchens. Even the name "sandwich" has branched out to include such things as burgers, subs and the very trendy wraps. As well, global influences have brought us such treats as falafels and pitas from the Middle East, fajitas and burritos from Mexico and pizza and calzones from Italy.

Sandwiches can be grilled, toasted, broiled, baked or chilled. They can be rolled, layered, stuffed or left "open-faced." Many can be made ahead and frozen to be thawed and heated, or just thawed, ready to be eaten as is. Mix and match recipes in the Sandwich Fillings section with the variety of yeast breads and flatbreads in the Breads section. Try Tangy Beef Spread tucked in between slices of Whole Wheat Batter Bread.

Put a Cream Cheese And Grape Jelly Sandwich in a school lunch bag or have a Chicken Submarine ready in the refrigerator when your child arrives home at noon. Let a hot Grilled Raisin And Cheese fill the hunger gap after school before supper. And on the weekend, for a casual Saturday supper, serve Loaf Of Pizza or Ham And Cheese Calzones. A platter of Pizza Pop-Ups will satisfy the teen party crowd. For Sunday brunch, Muffuletta will wow everyone—and satisfy their hunger at the same time! *Sandwiches And Wraps* will take the guesswork out of bag lunches, hot lunches, special luncheons and weekend brunches.

each recipe

has been analyzed using the most updated version of the Canadian Nutrient File from Health Canada, which is based upon the United States Department of Agriculture (USDA) Nutrient Data Base.

Margaret Ng, B.Sc. (Hon), M.A.
Registered Dietician

Breads

read is what makes a sandwich. Without it, we would have quite a mess on (or in) our hands!

Take your favorite filling and place it between fresh, warm slices of Pumpernickel Bread, page 9, or Rye Batter Bread, page 10—a different taste sensation every time. Did you know you can make your own Bagels, page 19, or Two-Hour Buns, on this page? Instead of the usual sandwich, make your own Basic Pizza Crust, page 13, Whole Wheat Pitas, page 11, or Flour Tortillas, page 16. This impressive collection of bread-type recipes will give you a never-ending choice of sandwich ideas.

TWO-HOUR BUNS

Makes a nice big batch—and yet so quick.

All-purpose flour	4 cups	1 L
Instant yeast	2 tbsp.	30 mL
Large eggs	2	2
Cooking oil	½ cup	125 mL
Water	3 cups	750 mL
Salt	1 tsp.	5 mL
All-purpose flour, approximately	5 cups	1.25 L
Hard margarine, softened	2 tsp.	10 mL

Combine first amount of flour and yeast in large bowl.

Beat eggs, cooking oil and water in medium bowl. Add to flour mixture. Add salt. Mix well.

Work in enough of second amount of flour until dough pulls away from sides of bowl. Cover with tea towel. Let stand in oven with light on and door closed for 15 minutes. Punch dough down. Shape into 48 egg-size buns. Place on 2 greased 9 x 13 inch (22 x 33 cm) pans. Cover with tea towel. Let stand in oven with light on and door closed for about 45 minutes until doubled in size. Bake in 350°F (175°C) oven for 25 to 30 minutes. Turn out onto racks to cool.

Brush warm tops with margarine. Makes 48.

1 bun: 117 Calories; 3 g Total Fat; 62 mg Sodium; 3 g Protein; 19 g Carbohydrate; 1 g Dietary Fiber

Pictured on page 17.

NUTRI BATTER BREAD

A good nutty taste. Quite a coarse texture.

Granulated sugar	1 tsp.	5 mL
Warm water	1¼ cups	300 mL
Active dry yeast	1 tbsp.	15 mL
Milk, scalded and cooled to lukewarm	1 cup	250 mL
Quick-cooking rolled oats (not instant)	¼ cup	60 mL
Natural bran (not cereal)	¼ cup	60 mL
Wheat germ	¼ cup	60 mL
Mild molasses	3 tbsp.	50 mL
Hard margarine, softened	2 tbsp.	30 mL
Salt	2 tsp.	10 mL
Large egg	1	1
Whole wheat flour	2 cups	500 mL
Sunflower (or sesame) seeds	¼ cup	60 mL
All-purpose flour	1 cup	250 mL
All-purpose flour	1½ cups	375 mL
Hard margarine, softened	2 tsp.	10 mL

Stir sugar in warm water in small bowl until sugar is dissolved. Sprinkle yeast over top. Let stand for 10 minutes. Stir until yeast is dissolved.

Combine next 8 ingredients in large bowl. Beat. Add yeast mixture. Beat well.

Beat in whole wheat flour. Add sunflower seeds and first amount of all-purpose flour. Beat in. Cover with greased waxed paper and tea towel. Let stand in oven with light on and door closed for about 45 minutes until doubled in size. Stir batter down.

Add second amount of all-purpose flour. Mix well. Spoon into 2 greased 9 x 5 x 3 inch (22 x 12.5 x 7.5 cm) loaf pans. Cover with greased waxed paper and tea towel. Let stand in oven with light on and door closed for about 1 hour until doubled in size. Bake in 350°F (175°C) oven for about 30 minutes. Turn out onto racks to cool.

Brush warm tops with second amount of margarine. Makes 2 loaves. Each loaf cuts into 18 slices, for a total of 36.

1 slice: 88 Calories; 2 g Total Fat; 167 mg Sodium; 3 g Protein; 15 g Carbohydrate; 2 g Dietary Fiber

Pictured on page 17.

For a shiny, moist crust, brush warm buns or bread with melted margarine (or butter) shortly after removal from the oven.

PUMPERNICKEL BREAD

Dark round loaves. Solid texture and excellent flavor.

Warm water	½ cup	125 mL
Granulated sugar	2 tbsp.	30 mL
Active dry yeast	3 tbsp.	50 mL
Mild molasses	⅓ cup	75 mL
Hard margarine, softened	2 tbsp.	30 mL
Salt	1 tbsp.	15 mL
Caraway seed (optional)	2 tbsp.	30 mL
Hot water	1¼ cups	300 mL
Rye flour (light or dark)	2½ cups	625 mL
Cocoa	¼ cup	60 mL
All-purpose flour, approximately	3 cups	750 mL
Hard margarine, softened	2 tsp.	10 mL

Stir warm water and sugar in small bowl until sugar is dissolved. Sprinkle yeast over top. Let stand for 10 minutes. Stir until yeast is dissolved.

Measure molasses, first amount of margarine, salt, caraway seed and hot water into large bowl. Stir. Cool to lukewarm.

Add rye flour and cocoa. Beat to mix thoroughly. Add yeast mixture. Stir.

Add about ½ of all-purpose flour. Mix. Work in enough of remaining flour until dough pulls away from sides of bowl. Turn out onto floured surface. Knead for 8 to 10 minutes until smooth and elastic. Place in large greased bowl, turning once to grease top. Cover with tea towel. Let stand in oven with light on and door closed for 45 to 60 minutes until doubled in size. Punch dough down. Divide dough into 2 equal portions. Shape into round balls. Place on greased baking sheets. Cover with tea towel. Let stand in oven with light on and door closed for 1 to 1½ hours until doubled in size. Bake in 375°F (190°C) oven for about 30 minutes. Turn out onto racks to cool.

Brush warm tops with second amount of margarine. Makes 2 loaves. Each loaf cuts into 12 wedges, for a total of 24.

1 wedge: 133 Calories; 1.8 g Total Fat; 308 mg Sodium; 3 g Protein; 27 g Carbohydrate; 3 g Dietary Fiber

For a chewy crust, brush loaves with water 2 or 3 times while baking. Omit brushing with margarine after removing from oven.

RYE BATTER BREAD

A good, easy bread. Dense in texture.

Granulated sugar	1 tsp.	5 mL
Warm water	¼ cup	60 mL
Active dry yeast	1 tbsp.	15 mL
Milk, scalded and cooled to lukewarm	1 cup	250 mL
Brown sugar, packed	3 tbsp.	50 mL
Hard margarine, softened	3 tbsp.	50 mL
Salt	1½ tsp.	7 mL
All-purpose flour	1½ cups	375 mL
Rye flour (light or dark)	1 cup	250 mL
All-purpose flour	½ cup	125 mL
Hard margarine, softened	1 tsp.	5 mL

Stir granulated sugar in warm water in small bowl until sugar is dissolved. Sprinkle yeast over top. Let stand for 10 minutes. Stir until yeast is dissolved.

Combine milk, brown sugar, first amount of margarine and salt in large bowl. Add yeast mixture. Stir.

Add first amount of all-purpose flour. Beat on low to moisten. Beat on medium for about 2 minutes until smooth.

Add rye flour and second amount of all-purpose flour. Beat well. Cover with greased waxed paper and tea towel. Let stand in oven with light on and door closed for about 1 hour until doubled in size. Work batter down. Turn into greased 1½ quart (1.5 L) casserole. Cover with greased waxed paper and tea towel. Let stand in oven with light on and door closed for 30 minutes until doubled in size. Bake in 375°F (190°C) oven for about 30 minutes. Turn out onto rack to cool.

Brush warm top with second amount of margarine. Makes 1 loaf. Cuts into 12 wedges.

1 wedge: 167 Calories; 3.9 g Total Fat; 390 mg Sodium; 4 g Protein; 29 g Carbohydrate; 2 g Dietary Fiber

Place frozen bread loaves and rolls in brown paper bag and put into 325°F (160°C) oven for 5 minutes to thaw completely.

ANADAMA BATTER BREAD

A large loaf. Fine-textured and a yellowish color.

Yellow cornmeal	½ cup	125 mL
Boiling water	1 cup	250 mL
Hard margarine	2 tbsp.	30 mL
Mild molasses	¼ cup	60 mL
Salt	1 tsp.	5 mL
Granulated sugar	1 tsp.	5 mL
Warm water	¼ cup	60 mL
Active dry yeast	1 tbsp.	15 mL
Large egg	1	1
All-purpose flour	2¾ cups	675 mL
Hard margarine, softened	1 tsp.	5 mL

Measure cornmeal into large bowl. Add boiling water. Stir.

Add next 3 ingredients. Stir until margarine is melted. Cool to lukewarm.

Stir sugar in warm water in small bowl until sugar is dissolved. Sprinkle yeast over top. Let stand for 10 minutes. Stir until yeast is dissolved. Add to cornmeal mixture. Stir.

Beat in egg. Beat in flour gradually. Cover with greased waxed paper and tea towel. Let stand in oven with light on and door closed for about 1¼ hours until doubled in size. Stir batter down. Place in greased 9 x 5 x 3 inch (22 x 12.5 x 7.5 cm) loaf pan. Cover with greased waxed paper and tea towel. Let stand in oven with light on and door closed for about 45 minutes until doubled in size. Bake in 375°F (190°C) oven for 30 to 35 minutes. Turn out onto rack to cool.

Brush warm top with second amount of margarine. Makes 1 loaf. Cuts into 18 slices.

1 slice: 121 Calories; 2.1 g Total Fat; 174 mg Sodium; 3 g Protein; 22 g Carbohydrate; 1 g Dietary Fiber

Pictured on page 17.

WHOLE WHEAT PITAS

Cut in half and fill "pockets" for a sandwich, or cut into pieces and serve as "crackers."

Whole wheat flour	2 cups	500 mL
Active dry yeast	1 tbsp.	15 mL
Warm water	1¼ cups	300 mL
Salt	½ tsp.	2 mL
All-purpose flour, approximately	1½ cups	375 mL

Measure first 4 ingredients into large bowl. Mix well.

Work in enough of all-purpose flour until dough pulls away from sides of bowl. Turn out onto floured surface. Knead for 4 to 5 minutes until smooth and elastic. Cut and shape into 10 balls. Roll out each ball ¼ inch (6 mm) thick and 5 to 6 inches (12.5 to 15 cm) in diameter on lightly floured surface. Both sides should be lightly covered with flour. Place on ungreased non-stick baking sheet or cornmeal-dusted baking sheet. Cover with tea towel. Let stand in oven with light on and door closed for about 35 minutes. Bake on bottom rack in 500°F (260°C) oven for 5 minutes. Repeat until all are baked. Wrap in tea towel for 3 minutes as they are removed from oven. Cool. Makes 10.

1 pita: 161 Calories; 0.7 g Total Fat; 138 mg Sodium; 6 g Protein; 34 g Carbohydrate; 4 g Dietary Fiber

OATMEAL BATTER BREAD

A light and flavorful loaf.

Rolled oats (not instant)	²/₃ cup	150 mL
Boiling water	1¼ cups	300 mL
Fancy molasses	¼ cup	60 mL
Hard margarine, softened	2 tbsp.	30 mL
Salt	1 tsp.	5 mL
Granulated sugar	1 tsp.	5 mL
Warm water	¼ cup	60 mL
Active dry yeast	1 tbsp.	15 mL
Large egg	1	1
All-purpose flour	3 cups	750 mL
Hard margarine, softened	2 tsp.	10 mL

Measure rolled oats into large bowl. Pour boiling water over rolled oats. Stir.

Add molasses, first amount of margarine and salt. Stir well. Cool to lukewarm.

Stir sugar in warm water in small bowl until sugar is dissolved. Sprinkle yeast over top. Let stand for 10 minutes. Stir until yeast is dissolved. Add to oat mixture.

Beat in egg. Beat in flour. Cover with greased waxed paper and tea towel. Let stand in oven with light on and door closed for about 1 hour until doubled in size. Stir batter down. Spoon into 2 greased 8 x 4 x 3 inch (20 x 10 x 7.5 cm) loaf pans. Cover with greased waxed paper and tea towel. Let stand in oven with light on and door closed for 35 to 45 minutes until doubled in size. Bake in 375°F (190°C) oven for about 35 minutes. Turn out onto racks to cool.

Brush warm tops with second amount of margarine. Makes 2 loaves. Each loaf cuts into 16 slices, for a total of 32.

1 slice: *71 Calories; 1.4 g Total Fat; 99 mg Sodium; 2 g Protein; 13 g Carbohydrate; 1 g Dietary Fiber*

WHOLE WHEAT BATTER BREAD

This tasty dense loaf is quick and easy. No kneading or rising time.

Granulated sugar	1 tsp.	5 mL
Warm water	½ cup	125 mL
Active dry yeast	1 tbsp.	15 mL
Whole wheat flour	4 cups	1 L
Brown sugar, packed	1 tbsp.	15 mL
Salt	1 tsp.	5 mL
Natural bran (not cereal)	¼ cup	60 mL
Wheat germ, toasted	¼ cup	60 mL
Warm water	1½ cups	375 mL
Cooking oil	¼ cup	60 mL
Hard margarine, softened	1 tsp.	5 mL

Stir sugar in first amount of warm water in small bowl until sugar is dissolved. Sprinkle yeast over top. Let stand for 10 minutes. Stir until yeast is dissolved.

Measure next 5 ingredients into large bowl. Add yeast mixture. Stir well.

Add second amount of warm water and cooking oil. Stir. Dough will be sticky and soft. Spoon evenly into greased 9 x 5 x 3 inch (22 x 12.5 x 7.5 cm) loaf pan. Bake in 375°F (190°C) oven for about 45 minutes. Turn out onto rack to cool.

Brush warm top with margarine. Makes 1 loaf. Cuts into 18 slices.

1 slice: *140 Calories; 4.2 g Total Fat; 155 mg Sodium; 5 g Protein; 23 g Carbohydrate; 4 g Dietary Fiber*

BASIC PIZZA CRUST

A crust that will work for any regular pizza.

All-purpose flour	2 cups	500 mL
Instant yeast	1¼ tsp.	6 mL
Salt	¼ tsp.	1 mL
Warm water	⅔ cup	150 mL
Cooking oil	2 tbsp.	30 mL

Food Processor Method: Put first 3 ingredients into food processor fitted with dough blade.

With machine running, pour warm water and cooking oil through tube in lid. Process for 50 to 60 seconds. If dough seems sticky to remove, add about ½ tsp. (2 mL) flour to make it easier to handle.

Hand Method: Put first 3 ingredients into medium bowl. Stir together well.

Add warm water and cooking oil. Mix well until dough leaves sides of bowl. Turn out onto floured surface. Knead for 5 to 8 minutes until smooth and elastic.

To Complete: At this point you may choose to roll out and press in greased 12 inch (30 cm) pizza pan, forming rim around edge. Or place dough in large greased bowl, turning once to grease top. Cover with tea towel. Let stand in oven with light on and door closed for about 1 hour until doubled in size. Punch dough down. Roll out and press in greased 12 inch (30 cm) pizza pan, forming rim around edge. Makes enough dough for 1 crust.

*⅛ **crust:** 153 Calories; 3.8 g Total Fat; 86 mg Sodium; 4 g Protein; 25 g Carbohydrate; 1 g Dietary Fiber*

TACO PIZZA CRUST: Mix ½ envelope of 1¼ oz. (35 g) taco seasoning mix into dry ingredients before adding wet ingredients.

THIN BASIC PIZZA CRUST: Reduce flour to 1½ cups (375 mL) and reduce water to ½ cup (125 mL). Crust will cook a bit quicker.

CALZONE PIZZA CRUST: Use Basic Pizza Crust or other crust as long as 2 cups (500 mL) flour are used. Makes 4 calzones.

BISCUIT MIX PIZZA CRUST

No crust is faster and easier.

Tea biscuit mix	2 cups	500 mL
Milk, approximately	½ cup	125 mL

Measure biscuit mix into medium bowl. Add slightly less milk at first, stirring to form soft ball. If too dry, add a bit more. Turn out onto lightly floured surface. Roll out and press in greased 12 inch (30 cm) pizza pan, forming rim around edge. Makes enough dough for 1 crust.

*⅛ **crust:** 150 Calories; 4.4 g Total Fat; 448 mg Sodium; 3 g Protein; 24 g Carbohydrate; 1 g Dietary Fiber*

BISCUIT PIZZA CRUST

Quicker to prepare than a yeast crust.

All-purpose flour	2 cups	500 mL
Baking powder	1 tbsp.	15 mL
Salt	¼ tsp.	1 mL
Water	⅔ cup	150 mL
Cooking oil	1 tbsp.	15 mL

Stir flour, baking powder and salt in medium bowl.

Add water and cooking oil. Stir to form soft ball. Turn out onto floured surface. Knead 8 to 10 times. Roll out and press in greased 12 inch (30 cm) pizza pan, forming rim around edge. Makes enough dough for 1 crust.

⅛ crust: 138 Calories; 2.1 g Total Fat; 92 mg Sodium; 3 g Protein; 26 g Carbohydrate; 1 g Dietary Fiber

THIN BISCUIT PIZZA CRUST: Reduce flour to 1½ cups (375 mL). Reduce water to ½ cup (125 mL). Crust will cook a bit quicker.

WHEAT BISCUIT PIZZA CRUST: Use whole wheat flour for half of all-purpose flour called for.

WHOLE WHEAT PIZZA CRUST

Tasty way to add fiber to your diet.

Whole wheat flour	1 cup	250 mL
All-purpose flour	1 cup	250 mL
Granulated sugar	½ tsp.	2 mL
Salt	¼ tsp.	1 mL
Instant yeast	1¼ tsp.	6 mL
Warm water	¾ cup	175 mL
Cooking oil	2 tbsp.	30 mL

Food Processor Method: Put first 5 ingredients into food processor fitted with dough blade.

With machine running, pour warm water and cooking oil through tube in lid. Process for 50 to 60 seconds. If dough seems sticky to remove, add about ½ tsp. (2 mL) flour to make it easier to handle.

Hand Method: Put first 5 ingredients into medium bowl. Stir together well.

Add warm water and cooking oil. Mix well until dough leaves sides of bowl. Turn out onto lightly floured surface. Knead for 5 to 8 minutes until smooth and elastic.

To Complete: At this point you may choose to roll out and press in greased 12 inch (30 cm) pizza pan, forming rim around edge. Or place dough in large greased bowl, turning once to grease top. Cover with tea towel. Let stand in oven with light on and door closed for about 1 hour until doubled in size. Punch dough down. Roll out and press in greased 12 inch (30 cm) pizza pan, forming rim around edge. Makes enough dough for 1 crust.

⅛ crust: 147 Calories; 3.9 g Total Fat; 86 mg Sodium; 4 g Protein; 25 g Carbohydrate; 3 g Dietary Fiber

RYE PIZZA CRUST

This crust is perfect for Reuben Pizza, page 49.

All-purpose flour	1 cup	250 mL
Rye flour (light or dark)	1 cup	250 mL
Granulated sugar	1 tsp.	5 mL
Salt	¼ tsp.	1 mL
Instant yeast	2½ tsp.	12 mL
Fancy molasses	2 tbsp.	30 mL
Warm water	⅔ cup	150 mL
Cooking oil	2 tbsp.	30 mL

Food Processor Method: Put first 5 ingredients into food processor fitted with dough blade.

Stir molasses into warm water in small bowl. With machine running, pour molasses mixture and cooking oil through tube in lid. Process for 50 to 60 seconds.

Hand Method: Put first 5 ingredients into medium bowl. Stir well.

Add molasses, warm water and cooking oil. Mix well until dough leaves sides of bowl. Turn out onto lightly floured surface. Knead for 6 to 8 minutes until smooth and elastic.

To Complete: At this point you may choose to roll out and press in greased 12 inch (30 cm) pizza pan, forming rim around edge. Or place dough in large greased bowl, turning once to grease top. Cover with tea towel. Let stand in oven with light on and door closed for about 1 hour until doubled in size. Punch dough down. Roll out and press in greased 12 inch (30 cm) pizza pan, forming rim around edge. Makes enough dough for 1 crust.

⅛ crust: 157 Calories; 3.9 g Total Fat; 87 mg Sodium; 3 g Protein; 27 g Carbohydrate; 3 g Dietary Fiber

CONFETTI BISCUIT PIZZA CRUST

Adds interest to any pizza with red and green flecks peeking out.

All-purpose flour	2 cups	500 mL
Baking powder	4 tsp.	20 mL
Granulated sugar	2 tsp.	10 mL
Salt	½ tsp.	2 mL
Chopped green pepper	¼ cup	60 mL
Chopped red pepper	¼ cup	60 mL
Chopped green onion	¼ cup	60 mL
Parsley flakes	1 tsp.	5 mL
Cooking oil	¼ cup	60 mL
Milk	½ cup	125 mL

Measure first 8 ingredients into medium bowl. Mix well.

Add cooking oil and milk. Stir to form soft ball. Turn out onto lightly floured surface. Knead 8 times. Roll out and press in greased 12 inch (30 cm) pizza pan, forming rim around edge. Makes enough dough for 1 crust.

⅛ crust: 202 Calories; 7.8 g Total Fat; 188 mg Sodium; 4 g Protein; 29 g Carbohydrate; 1 g Dietary Fiber

SWEDISH POCKETS

Cut in half and fill pockets with tomato slices, cheese slices or cold meats. Or cut into wedges and eat as a snack.

Buttermilk (or reconstituted from powder)	2¹/₂ cups	625 mL
Hard margarine, softened	¹/₂ cup	125 mL
Salt	1 tbsp.	15 mL
Granulated sugar	1 tsp.	5 mL
Warm water	¹/₄ cup	60 mL
Active dry yeast	2 tbsp.	30 mL
Rye flour (light or dark)	2 cups	500 mL
All-purpose flour	4¹/₂ cups	1.1 L

Scald buttermilk in small saucepan. Remove from heat. Add margarine and salt. Stir until margarine is melted. Cool to lukewarm.

Stir sugar in warm water in large bowl until sugar is dissolved. Sprinkle yeast over top. Let stand for 10 minutes. Stir until yeast is dissolved. Add buttermilk mixture. Stir.

Add rye flour. Stir. Add all-purpose flour. Stir. Turn out onto floured surface. Knead for 8 to 10 minutes until smooth and elastic. Place in large greased bowl, turning once to grease top. Cover with greased waxed paper and tea towel. Let stand for at least 8 hours or overnight. Shape into egg-size balls. Roll out each ball ¹/₄ inch (6 mm) thick and 4 inches (10 cm) in diameter. Arrange on ungreased baking sheets. Bake in 400°F (205°C) oven for 10 to 12 minutes until golden. Remove to racks to cool. Cover immediately with tea towel or place in paper bag to retain softness. Makes 36.

1 pocket: *114 Calories; 3.2 g Total Fat; 245 mg Sodium; 3 g Protein; 18 g Carbohydrate; 1 g Dietary Fiber*

FLOUR TORTILLAS

Easy to make. Try Cucumber Under Wraps, page 60, or Speedy Fajitas, page 115.

All-purpose flour	2 cups	500 mL
Baking powder	1 tsp.	5 mL
Salt	1 tsp.	5 mL
Hard margarine	¹/₄ cup	60 mL
Water	²/₃ cup	150 mL

Place flour, baking powder and salt in medium bowl. Cut in margarine until crumbly.

Add water. Stir until dough forms a ball, adding more water, 1 tbsp. (15 mL) at a time, if necessary. Turn out onto floured surface. Knead 6 to 8 times. Cover with inverted bowl. Let rest for 20 minutes. Roll out a portion as thin as you can. Invert 7 inch (18 cm) bowl or 8 inch (20 cm) plate onto dough. Cut around edge. Repeat until all dough is used. Place 1 tortilla on hot, ungreased medium frying pan. Some dark spots will appear in 15 to 20 seconds. Turn over. Brown for 15 to 20 seconds on second side until there are some dark spots. Keep warm in tea towel. Cool and wrap airtight to store. Makes 10.

1 tortilla: *141 Calories; 5.2 g Total Fat; 331 mg Sodium; 3 g Protein; 20 g Carbohydrate; 1 g Dietary Fiber*

1. Olive Nut Filling, page 65
2. Shrimp Cream Spread, page 67
3. Two-Hour Buns, page 7
4. Tangy Beef Spread, page 67
5. Egg Filling, page 63
6. Anadama Batter Bread, page 11
7. Cream Fruit Spread, page 65
8. Nutri Batter Bread, page 8

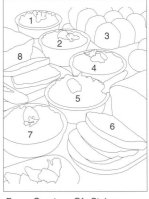

Props Courtesy Of: Stokes
The Bay

BAGELS

Cut in half and toast, serve with flavored cream cheese or broil each half with Cheddar cheese. The possibilities are endless!

Granulated sugar	1 tsp.	5 mL
Warm water	¾ cup	175 mL
Active dry yeast	1 tbsp.	15 mL
Large eggs	2	2
Cooking oil	2 tbsp.	30 mL
All-purpose flour	2 cups	500 mL
Granulated sugar	1 tbsp.	15 mL
Salt	1¾ tsp.	9 mL
All-purpose flour, approximately	1½ cups	375 mL

POACHING LIQUID

Water	4 quarts	4 L
Granulated sugar	2 tbsp.	30 mL

TOPPING

Large egg, fork-beaten	1	1
Sesame (or poppy) seeds (optional)		

Stir first amount of sugar in warm water in large bowl until sugar is dissolved. Sprinkle yeast over top. Let stand for 10 minutes. Stir until yeast is dissolved.

Whisk in eggs and cooking oil. Beat in first amount of flour, second amount of sugar and salt until smooth.

Work in enough of second amount of flour to make a soft dough. Turn out onto floured surface. Knead for 8 to 10 minutes until dough is smooth and elastic. Place in large greased bowl, turning once to grease top. Cover with tea towel. Let stand in oven with light on and door closed for 1 to 1½ hours until doubled in size. Punch dough down. Divide into 12 equal portions. Roll each portion into 10 inch (25 cm) rope. Cover remaining portions with damp tea towel while rolling and shaping each rope. Bring ends of rope together, overlapping slightly. Pinch end to firmly seal. Place on floured baking sheet. Cover with tea towel. Let stand in oven with light on and door closed for 15 minutes.

Poaching Liquid: Bring water to a boil in large saucepan. Add sugar. Reduce heat to medium to keep water at a slow boil. Slip bagels into water, 3 or 4 at a time. Poach for 1 minute. Turn. Poach for 1 minute. Remove bagels to well-greased baking sheets.

Topping: Brush egg over top of each bagel. Sprinkle with sesame seeds. Bake in 400°F (205°C) oven for 20 to 25 minutes or until golden brown. Place on racks to cool. Makes 12.

1 bagel: 187 Calories; 4 g Total Fat; 413 mg Sodium; 6 g Protein; 31 g Carbohydrate; 1 g Dietary Fiber

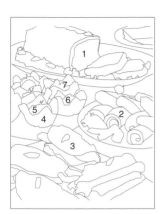

1. Sandwich Loaf, page 38
2. Crab Rolls, page 58
3. Cheese Puffs, page 48
4. Toast Cups, page 105
5. Smoked Salmon Filling, page 67
6. Cucumber Filling, page 63
7. Crunchy Egg Filling, page 63

Props Courtesy Of: Stokes

Burgers & Buns

hamburger is probably the most classic and popular of these sandwiches, but almost anything can be slipped in between a bun and served with style. Take a moment to glance through these recipes and you'll be inspired to try something a little different, like Apple Burgers, page 21, or Beef And Avocado Sandwiches, page 24. And don't limit yourself to hamburger buns. Try the great variety of rolls and buns that are available nowadays, or make your own Two-Hour Buns, page 7.

BEAN BURGERS

Sensational with fried onion, ketchup and relish.

Can of beans in tomato sauce	14 oz.	398 mL
Grated sharp Cheddar cheese	¾ cup	175 mL
Dry bread crumbs	1½ cups	375 mL
Large egg, fork-beaten	1	1
Liquid gravy browner	1 tsp.	5 mL
Soy sauce	2 tsp.	10 mL
Bulgur	¼ cup	60 mL
Boiling water	¼ cup	60 mL
Cooking oil	1 tbsp.	15 mL
Margarine	⅓ cup	75 mL
Hamburger buns, split	8	8

Mash beans in medium bowl.

Mix in cheese, bread crumbs, egg, gravy browner and soy sauce. Let stand for 10 minutes.

Combine bulgur and boiling water in small bowl. Cover. Let stand for 15 minutes. Add to bean mixture. Shape into patties, using about ¼ cup (60 mL) for each.

Heat cooking oil in frying pan. Add patties. Brown on both sides.

Spread margarine on both halves of buns. Insert patties. Makes 8.

1 burger: 365 Calories; 8.2 g Total Fat; 817 mg Sodium; 14 g Protein; 55 g Carbohydrate; 5 g Dietary Fiber

Pictured on page 107.

APPLE BURGERS

Try topping the patty with applesauce instead of mustard and ketchup.

Lean ground chicken (or turkey)	1 lb.	454 g
Applesauce	$\frac{1}{2}$ cup	125 mL
Finely chopped onion	2 tbsp.	30 mL
Finely chopped green or red pepper	2 tbsp.	30 mL
Seasoned salt	$\frac{3}{4}$ tsp.	4 mL
Pepper	$\frac{1}{8}$ tsp.	0.5 mL
Margarine	$\frac{1}{4}$ cup	60 mL
Hamburger buns, split	6	6

Mix first 6 ingredients in small bowl. Divide mixture into 6 equal portions. Form each portion into a patty. Place on ungreased broiler tray. Broil for 8 minutes. Turn patties over. Broil for 8 minutes until patties are lightly browned and no longer pink inside.

Spread margarine on both halves of buns. Insert patties. Makes 6.

1 burger: 301 Calories; 12.6 g Total Fat; 564 mg Sodium; 19 g Protein; 27 g Carbohydrate; 1 g Dietary Fiber

CHICKEN BURGERS

These are delicious and different, especially with cranberry sauce. Also excellent with bacon, avocado, tomato, salad dressing and alfalfa sprouts added. Try the works!

Ground chicken	1 lb.	454 g
Dry bread crumbs	$\frac{1}{4}$ cup	60 mL
Milk (or water)	$\frac{1}{4}$ cup	60 mL
Salt	1 tsp.	5 mL
Pepper	$\frac{1}{4}$ tsp.	1 mL
Margarine	$2\frac{1}{2}$ tbsp.	37 mL
Hamburger buns, split	4	4

Mix first 5 ingredients in small bowl. Shape into 4 large patties. Fry in well-greased frying pan.

Spread margarine on both halves of buns. Insert patties. Makes 4.

1 burger: 358 Calories; 13.1 g Total Fat; 1146 mg Sodium; 28 g Protein; 30 g Carbohydrate; 1 g Dietary Fiber

To make sure a barbecued patty cooks all the way through, poke a hole in the center with your finger just before placing on grill. The hole will close up by the time the patty is cooked through.

TURKEY BURGERS

Serve with the usual burger condiments but either light mayonnaise or cranberry sauce is even better.

Ground turkey	1 lb.	454 g
Grated potato	1 cup	250 mL
Onion flakes	1 tbsp.	15 mL
Prepared horseradish	2 tsp.	10 mL
Liquid gravy browner	1/4 tsp.	1 mL
Parsley flakes	1/2 tsp.	2 mL
Salt	3/4 tsp.	4 mL
Pepper	1/8 tsp.	0.5 mL
Chicken bouillon powder	1 tsp.	5 mL
Cooking oil	1 tbsp.	15 mL
Margarine	1/4 cup	60 mL
Hamburger buns, split	6	6

Measure first 9 ingredients into small bowl. Mix. Shape into 6 patties.

Fry in cooking oil in frying pan, browning both sides until no pink remains in turkey.

Spread margarine on both halves of buns. Insert patties. Makes 6.

1 burger: 336 Calories; 14.2 g Total Fat; 840 mg Sodium; 21 g Protein; 30 g Carbohydrate; 1 g Dietary Fiber

---

If potato chips lose their freshness, spread them on a baking sheet and place under the broiler for a few moments, watching them carefully so they don't brown.

BEEF DIP SANDWICHES

These are a lot of fun to eat. Beef-filled rolls are dipped into a tasty beef gravy. Have paper napkins handy!

Rump (or sirloin tip) roast	3 lbs.	1.4 kg
Water		
Beef bouillon powder	1 tbsp.	15 mL
Garlic powder	1/4 tsp.	1 mL
Onion powder	1/4 tsp.	1 mL
Worcestershire sauce	1/2 tsp.	2 mL
Salt, sprinkle (optional)		
Pepper	1/4 tsp.	1 mL
Day-old french rolls, split	6	6

Place roast in small roaster. Pour water into roaster halfway up roast. Cover. Bake in 400°F (205°C) oven for 15 minutes. Reduce heat to 275°F (140°C). Bake for 3 to 3 1/2 hours until very tender. Remove roast to plate. Cover to keep warm.

Measure liquid from roaster. You should have about 4 cups (1 L). Add hot water, if needed, to bring measurement up to 4 cups (1 L). Add next 4 ingredients. Stir. Taste for salt. Add pepper. Stir. Divide among 6 bowls.

Slice roast and fill rolls. Serve with gravy for dipping. Makes 6.

1 sandwich (without gravy): 470 Calories; 11.6 g Total Fat; 763 mg Sodium; 57 g Protein; 30 g Carbohydrate; 1 g Dietary Fiber

Pictured on page 53 and back cover.

SURPRISE BURGERS

Prepare and cook in 30 minutes. There's a surprise in the middle!

Lean ground beef	1 lb.	454 g
Large egg	1	1
Chopped cooked spinach, squeezed dry	3 tbsp.	50 mL
Grated onion	1 tbsp.	15 mL
Salt	½ tsp.	2 mL
Freshly ground pepper, to taste		
Grated medium Cheddar cheese	3 tbsp.	50 mL
Light salad dressing (or mayonnaise), for garnish		
Ketchup, for garnish		
Kaiser rolls (or buns), split and toasted	4	4
Ripe medium tomato slices	4	4

Combine first 6 ingredients in medium bowl. Divide into 4 large and 4 small portions. Form large portions into patties. Make indentation in center of each.

Fill each with ¼ of cheese. Flatten small portion of beef mixture. Seal over top of cheese. Broil or barbecue patties for 10 minutes until no longer pink inside.

Spread salad dressing and ketchup on bottom halves of rolls. Top with patty and tomato slice. Cover with top halves of rolls. Makes 4.

1 burger: 338 Calories; 13.9 g Total Fat; 648 mg Sodium; 27 g Protein; 25 g Carbohydrate; 1 g Dietary Fiber

BEEF VEGETABLE SANDWICHES

Ready in 20 minutes. Uses leftover cooked beef.

Plain yogurt	½ cup	125 mL
Grated carrot	½ cup	125 mL
Finely chopped onion	1 tbsp.	15 mL
Dried sweet basil	½ tsp.	2 mL
Kaiser rolls, split	4	4
Lettuce leaves	4	4
Large tomato, thinly sliced	1	1
Cooked lean beef, thinly sliced	8 oz.	225 g
Medium cucumber, peeled and thinly sliced	½	½
Grated medium Cheddar cheese	¼ cup	60 mL
Alfalfa sprouts	1 cup	250 mL
Salt, to taste		
Pepper, to taste		

Combine yogurt, carrot, onion, and basil in small bowl. Stir. Set aside.

Layer bottom halves of rolls with lettuce, tomato, beef, cucumber, cheese and alfalfa sprouts. Sprinkle with salt and pepper. Spoon ¼ cup (60 mL) yogurt mixture over top of sprouts. Cover with top halves of rolls. Makes 4.

1 sandwich: 300 Calories; 8.2 g Total Fat; 278 mg Sodium; 28 g Protein; 37 g Carbohydrate; 1 g Dietary Fiber

BEEF AND AVOCADO SANDWICHES

Serve immediately before avocado starts to turn color.

Packed fresh sweet basil leaves	1 cup	250 mL
Coarsely chopped fresh parsley	¼ cup	60 mL
Garlic cloves, halved	3	3
Coarsely chopped onion	¼ cup	60 mL
Ripe avocado, peeled and halved	1	1
Lemon juice	2 tbsp.	30 mL
Salt	½ tsp.	2 mL
Freshly ground pepper, to taste		
Olive oil	3 tbsp.	50 mL
Italian buns (or kaiser rolls), split	8	8
Deli (or cooked) lean beef, very thinly sliced	1 lb.	454 g
Large tomatoes, sliced	2	2
Red or green leafy lettuce leaves	8	8
Salt, to taste		
Freshly ground pepper, to taste		

Measure basil, parsley, garlic and onion into food processor. Process, scraping down sides occasionally, until finely minced.

Add avocado, lemon juice, salt, pepper and olive oil. Process until smooth. Remove mixture to medium bowl. Cover. Chill for 30 minutes to meld flavors.

Spread avocado mixture on bottom halves of buns. Layer beef, tomato and lettuce on top. Season with salt and pepper. Cover with top halves of buns. Makes 8.

1 sandwich: 356 Calories; 13.8 g Total Fat; 527 mg Sodium; 23 g Protein; 36 g Carbohydrate; 3 g Dietary Fiber

BENEDICT MUFFIN

Bacon, egg and cheese—they're all here—Eggs Benedict sandwich-style.

Margarine	2 tsp.	10 mL
English muffin, split and toasted	1	1
Canadian bacon slice, cooked	1	1
Large egg, fried firm	1	1
Salt, sprinkle		
Pepper, sprinkle		
Process cheese spread (optional)	2 tsp.	10 mL

Spread margarine on both halves of muffin. Layer bacon and egg on bottom half of muffin. Sprinkle with salt and pepper.

Spread cheese on top half of muffin. Place over egg. Serve hot. Makes 1.

1 muffin: 329 Calories; 16.1 g Total Fat; 698 mg Sodium; 17 g Protein; 28 g Carbohydrate; 1 g Dietary Fiber

Pictured on page 90.

Pepper Cheese Roll

Colored peppers make this a real treat. This can be made ahead, wrapped with plastic wrap and chilled for up to two days.

Whole wheat roll, oblong or oval-shaped (about 5 inches, 12.5 cm, long), split	1	1
Low-fat Italian dressing	1 tbsp.	15 mL
Red, orange or yellow pepper, cut into thin strips	1/2	1/2
Pepper, sprinkle		
Dried sweet basil, just a pinch		
Part-skim mozzarella (or Swiss or Monterey Jack) cheese, thinly sliced	2 oz.	57 g
Alfalfa sprouts (optional)	1/4 cup	60 mL

Remove bit of bread from soft center of top and bottom half of roll, making a slight hollow. Brush dressing on both halves of roll. Layer pepper strips lengthwise across bottom half. Sprinkle with pepper and basil. Lay cheese slices over top.

Spread alfalfa sprouts over cheese. Cover with top half of roll. Makes 1.

1 roll: 345 Calories; 11.7 g Total Fat; 322 mg Sodium; 21 g Protein; 42 g Carbohydrate; 5 g Dietary Fiber

Pictured on front cover.

Veggie Bagel

A messy, but delicious stacked sandwich that's ready in minutes!

Whole wheat (or multigrain) bagel, split	1	1
Plain (or herbed) spreadable cream cheese	1 tbsp.	15 mL
Cucumber slices, with peel	3-4	3-4
Medium tomato slice(s)	1-2	1-2
Salt, sprinkle		
Pepper, sprinkle		
Alfalfa sprouts (optional)	2 tbsp.	30 mL

Toast bagel halves until lightly browned.

Spread cream cheese on both halves. Layer cucumber and tomato slices on bottom half.

Sprinkle with salt and pepper. Spread alfalfa sprouts over tomato. Cover with top half of bagel. Cut in half. Makes 1.

1 bagel: 215 Calories; 6.3 g Total Fat; 314 mg Sodium; 8 g Protein; 36 g Carbohydrate; 3 g Dietary Fiber

MOCK LOBSTER ROLLS

A pinkish color. Serve filling in Italian rolls and add frilly lettuce leaves for a pretty luncheon presentation.

Haddock fillets (or steaks)	1 lb.	454 g
Water, to cover		
Chili sauce	2 tbsp.	30 mL
Prepared horseradish	1 tbsp.	15 mL
Finely chopped celery	1½ tbsp.	25 mL
Light salad dressing (or mayonnaise)	3 tbsp.	50 mL
Non-fat sour cream	2 tbsp.	30 mL
Salt	⅛ tsp.	0.5 mL
Margarine	⅓ cup	75 mL
Hot dog buns, split	8	8

Put haddock and water into small saucepan. Bring to a boil. Simmer gently for about 5 minutes until fish flakes easily. Drain. Cool slightly. Flake fish, discarding bones.

Mix next 6 ingredients in small bowl. Add fish. Stir. Makes 1½ cups (375 mL) filling.

Spread margarine on both halves of buns. Spread about 3 tbsp. (50 mL) filling on bottom halves. Cover with top halves. Makes 8.

1 roll: 274 Calories; 12 g Total Fat; 518 mg Sodium; 15 g Protein; 26 g Carbohydrate; 1 g Dietary Fiber

FISH BURGERS

While these call for salad dressing, you may choose to use tartar sauce.

Cod (or sole) fillets (about 1 lb., 454 g)	6	6
Lemon juice	1 tbsp.	15 mL
All-purpose flour	¼ cup	60 mL
Salt	1 tsp.	5 mL
Pepper	¼ tsp.	1 mL
Paprika	½ tsp.	2 mL
Seasoned salt	¼ tsp.	1 mL
Cooking oil, for deep-frying		
Margarine	¼ cup	60 mL
Hamburger buns, split and toasted	6	6
Light salad dressing (or mayonnaise)	2 tbsp.	30 mL
Lettuce leaves, left whole or chopped	6	6

Sprinkle fillets with lemon juice. Set aside.

Stir next 5 ingredients in small bowl. Coat fish fillets with flour mixture.

Deep-fry in hot 375°F (190°C) cooking oil for 3 to 4 minutes until golden.

Spread margarine on both halves of buns. Spread top halves with 1 tsp. (5 mL) salad dressing each. Place fish on bottom halves. Cover with folded lettuce leaves. Cover with top halves of buns. Makes 6.

1 burger: 347 Calories; 17 g Total Fat; 927 mg Sodium; 18 g Protein; 30 g Carbohydrate; 1 g Dietary Fiber

SALMON BURGERS

These nicely browned burgers are absolutely delicious.

Large egg, fork-beaten	1	1
Can of red salmon, drained, skin and round bones removed	7¹/₂ oz.	213 g
Parsley flakes	¹/₂ tsp.	2 mL
Dill weed	¹/₈ tsp.	0.5 mL
Salt	¹/₄ tsp.	1 mL
Onion powder	¹/₄ tsp.	1 mL
Dry bread crumbs	¹/₂ cup	125 mL
Water	¹/₄ cup	60 mL
Margarine	1 tbsp.	15 mL
Margarine	2¹/₂ tbsp.	37 mL
Hamburger buns, split	4	4

Mix first 6 ingredients in medium bowl.

Add bread crumbs and water. Stir well. Let stand for 5 minutes so bread crumbs can soak. Shape into 4 patties.

Melt first amount of margarine in frying pan. Add patties. Brown both sides.

Spread second amount of margarine on both halves of buns. Insert patties. Makes 4.

1 burger: 370 Calories; 17.3 g Total Fat; 898 mg Sodium; 18 g Protein; 35 g Carbohydrate; 1 g Dietary Fiber

TUNA BURGERS

Bits of celery manage to make an appearance through the top. Economy plus.

Large egg, fork-beaten	1	1
Can of tuna, drained and flaked	6¹/₂ oz.	184 g
Dry bread crumbs	¹/₂ cup	125 mL
Finely chopped celery	¹/₃ cup	75 mL
Finely chopped onion (or ¹/₄ tsp., 1 mL, powder)	¹/₃ cup	75 mL
Salt	¹/₄ tsp.	1 mL
Margarine	1 tbsp.	15 mL
Margarine	2¹/₂ tbsp.	37 mL
Hamburger buns, split	4	4

Mix egg, tuna, bread crumbs, celery, onion and salt in medium bowl. Let stand for 5 minutes. Shape into 4 patties.

Melt first amount of margarine in frying pan. Add patties. Brown both sides.

Spread second amount of margarine on both halves of buns. Insert patties. Makes 4.

1 burger: 358 Calories; 15.5 g Total Fat; 815 mg Sodium; 18 g Protein; 36 g Carbohydrate; 1 g Dietary Fiber

Cocktail Sandwiches

ocktail sandwiches are a wonderful finger food to offer during an afternoon tea, or as something a little more substantial than conventional appetizers for an evening function. Display them on an eye-catching platter in an artful arrangement, and don't be surprised if you receive more than a few "kudos" for your effort.

HAM PINWHEELS

Make one day ahead or make and freeze several weeks ahead.

Can of ham flakes, drained	6½ oz.	184 g
Light salad dressing (or mayonnaise)	3 tbsp.	50 mL
Worcestershire sauce	1 tbsp.	15 mL
Prepared mustard	1 tsp.	5 mL
Onion powder	¼ tsp.	1 mL
White (or whole wheat) unsliced bread loaf, sliced lengthwise by bakery	1	1
Margarine	3 tbsp.	50 mL
Gherkins, approximately	9	9

Mash first 5 ingredients in small bowl.

Remove crusts from 3 long slices of bread. Roll lightly with rolling pin. Spread 1 side of each slice with margarine. Spread ham mixture over margarine. Arrange gherkins, end to end, along short end of bread, over ham mixture. Roll bread up. Place, seam side down, in shallow container. Cover with damp tea towel. Chill. To serve, unwrap and slice into 12 slices per roll, for a total of 36.

1 slice: 59 Calories; 2.6 g Total Fat; 184 mg Sodium; 2 g Protein; 7 g Carbohydrate; trace Dietary Fiber

CHEESE FINERY

Make these ahead and chill.

Light salad dressing (or mayonnaise)	3 tbsp.	50 mL
Grated light sharp Cheddar cheese	2 cups	500 mL
Jars of sliced pimiento (2 oz., 57 mL, each), with liquid, chopped	2	2
Onion powder	$1/2$ tsp.	2 mL
Hot pepper sauce	$1/8$ tsp.	0.5 mL
Day-old dark bread slices	16	16
Day-old white bread slices	16	16
Margarine	$1/4$ cup	60 mL

Mix first 5 ingredients in medium bowl.

Cut three 1¾ inch (4.5 cm) circles from each bread slice. Spread margarine on 1 side of each bread circle. Divide filling over margarine on each dark bread circle. Top with white bread circles, buttered side down. Makes 48.

1 cocktail sandwich: 63 Calories; 2.7 g Total Fat; 125 mg Sodium; 3 g Protein; 7 g Carbohydrate; 1 g Dietary Fiber

BANANA PINWHEELS

One of the most popular party sandwiches.

Day-old unsliced sandwich bread loaf, sliced lengthwise by bakery	1	1
Margarine	$1/4$ cup	60 mL
Smooth peanut butter	$1/2$ cup	125 mL
Firm medium bananas	4	4
Dill pickle juice	2 tbsp.	30 mL

Remove crusts from each slice. Roll each slice lightly with rolling pin. Spread 1 side to edge with margarine. Spread to edge with peanut butter. Trim banana to width of bread slice. Brush banana with pickle juice. Lay on short end of bread and roll bread up. Wrap each roll and chill. To serve, unwrap and slice into 12 slices per roll, for a total of 48.

1 slice: 57 Calories; 2.7 g Total Fat; 84 mg Sodium; 2 g Protein; 7 g Carbohydrate; trace Dietary Fiber

RIBBON SANDWICHES

Always so desirable, and they look so attractive on a sandwich tray.

Day-old dark bread slices	4	4
Margarine	4 tsp.	20 mL
Day-old white bread slices	2	2
Cream Pepper Spread, page 64	2 tbsp.	30 mL
Crunchy Egg Filling, page 63	$1/4$ cup	60 mL

Spread 1 side of each dark bread slice with margarine. Spread both sides of white bread slices with margarine. Spread 2 slices of dark bread with Cream Pepper Spread. Cover with white bread slice. Spread top of white bread slice with Crunchy Egg Filling. Top with remaining 2 slices of dark bread, buttered side down. Wrap each stack. Chill. To serve, hold down stack and cut off crusts. Cut each stack into 6 slices. Cut each slice into 4 strips, for a total of 48.

1 cocktail sandwich: 15 Calories; 0.8 g Total Fat; 34 mg Sodium; trace Protein; 2 g Carbohydrate; trace Dietary Fiber

Pictured on page 72.

Tuna Towers

The unusual addition of grated apple gives these their good flavor.

Can of tuna, drained and flaked	6½ oz.	184 g
Grated apple, peeled	⅓ cup	75 mL
Finely chopped celery	¼ cup	60 mL
Sweet pickle relish	1 tsp.	5 mL
Onion powder	¼ tsp.	1 mL
Light salad dressing (or mayonnaise)	¼ cup	60 mL
Salt	⅛ tsp.	0.5 mL
Dark bread slices	18	18
Margarine	⅔ cup	150 mL
Pimiento-stuffed olive slices, for garnish	24	24

Mix first 7 ingredients in small bowl.

Cut four 1½ inch (3.8 cm) circles from each bread slice. Spread margarine and filling between layers to make 3-tiered sandwiches. Garnish with olive slices. Makes 24.

1 cocktail sandwich: 111 Calories; 6.6 g Total Fat; 235 mg Sodium; 4 g Protein; 10 g Carbohydrate; 1 g Dietary Fiber

Rainbow Sandwiches

Here is a plateful of colors to decorate your party table.

Light cream cheese, softened	8 oz.	250 g
Milk	4 tsp.	20 mL
Red, green and blue food coloring		
Day-old sandwich bread loaf slices (use white, whole wheat or both)	12	12
Margarine	¼ cup	60 mL

Mash cream cheese and milk together in small bowl. Divide into thirds in 3 small bowls. Add a few drops of red food coloring to 1 bowl to make a light pink. Repeat with green and blue in remaining 2 bowls, keeping both quite light.

Spread 1 side of bread slices with margarine. Spread 3 slices with pink filling, 3 slices with green filling and 3 slices with blue filling. Stack. Top with remaining 3 slices, buttered side down. Wrap each stack. Chill. To serve, hold down stack and cut off crusts. Cut each stack in half. Cut each half into 7 sandwiches, for a total of 42.

1 cocktail sandwich: 42 Calories; 2.4 g Total Fat; 109 mg Sodium; 1 g Protein; 4 g Carbohydrate; trace Dietary Fiber

To serve cocktail sandwiches, arrange them on a platter at angles to show off the layers.

Foil-Wrapped Sandwiches

f you'd like a warm meal, then consider one of these great recipes featuring sandwiches wrapped in foil and heated in the oven.

Among this selection are some ideas for subs, burgers and buns brimming with assorted fillings. The possibilities are endless!

TOASTY TUNA TORPEDOES

These can made ahead, frozen, and then baked for 25 to 30 minutes.

Can of tuna, drained and flaked	6½ oz.	184 g
Grated light Cheddar cheese	1 cup	250 mL
Chopped dill pickle	2 tbsp.	30 mL
Green onion, thinly sliced	1	1
Prepared mustard	1 tbsp.	15 mL
Light salad dressing (or mayonnaise)	1 tbsp.	15 mL
Hot dog buns, split	4	4

Combine tuna, cheese, pickle and green onion in small bowl.

Add mustard and salad dressing. Stir.

Spread bottom halves of buns with tuna mixture. Cover with top halves. Wrap each bun in foil. Bake in 350°F (175°C) oven for 15 minutes until heated through. Cool slightly before unwrapping. Makes 4.

1 bun: 296 Calories; 10.7 g Total Fat; 724 mg Sodium; 22 g Protein; 26 g Carbohydrate; 1 g Dietary Fiber

Pictured on page 35.

BBQ Chicken Buns

Serve these on the patio for good outdoor fun. But if the rain comes, head indoors—they'll still taste great!

Margarine	1 tsp.	5 mL
Finely chopped onion	1/2 cup	125 mL
Finely chopped celery	1/4 cup	60 mL
Water	1/2 cup	125 mL
Beef bouillon powder	1 tsp.	5 mL
Ketchup	1/2 cup	125 mL
White vinegar	2 tsp.	10 mL
Worcestershire sauce	1 tsp.	5 mL
Chili powder	1 tsp.	5 mL
Salt	1/2 tsp.	2 mL
Pepper	1/8 tsp.	0.5 mL
Chopped pimiento-stuffed olives	1/3 cup	75 mL
Chopped cooked chicken	3 cups	750 mL
Margarine	1/2 cup	125 mL
Kaiser rolls (or hamburger buns), split	12	12

Melt first amount of margarine in large frying pan. Add onion and celery. Sauté until soft.

Add next 10 ingredients. Stir. Heat through.

Spread second amount of margarine on both halves of rolls. Spread scant 1/4 cup (60 mL) filling on bottom halves. Cover with top halves. Wrap each roll in foil. Bake in 350°F (175°C) oven for about 15 minutes until heated through. Cool slightly before unwrapping. Makes 12.

1 bun: 313 Calories; 11.8 g Total Fat; 849 mg Sodium; 17 g Protein; 34 g Carbohydrate; 2 g Dietary Fiber

Pictured on page 35.

Oven Subs

These appetizing buns make a good quick lunch.

Margarine	1 tbsp.	15 mL
Chopped onion	1 1/4 cups	300 mL
Can of beans in tomato sauce	14 oz.	398 mL
Ketchup	1 tbsp.	15 mL
Salt, sprinkle		
Pepper, sprinkle		
Submarine buns, split	4	4
Grated medium or sharp Cheddar cheese	3/4 cup	175 mL

Melt margarine in frying pan. Add onion. Sauté until soft.

Add beans, ketchup, salt and pepper. Stir. Makes a generous 2 cups (500 mL) filling.

Spread bottom halves of buns with bean mixture. Sprinkle with cheese. Cover with top halves. Wrap each bun in foil. Bake in 350°F (175°C) oven for 15 minutes until heated through. Cool slightly before unwrapping. Makes 4.

1 bun: 513 Calories; 16.6 g Total Fat; 1145 mg Sodium; 19 g Protein; 74 g Carbohydrate; 9 g Dietary Fiber

TURKEY BUNWICHES

Eat these immediately or heat them in the oven later. A great way to use leftover turkey.

Margarine	1 tbsp.	15 mL
Water	2 tbsp.	30 mL
Sliced or chopped onion	1 cup	250 mL
Diced cooked turkey	2 cups	500 mL
Finely diced celery	½ cup	125 mL
Parsley flakes	1 tsp.	5 mL
Salt	¼ tsp.	1 mL
Pepper, sprinkle		
Light salad dressing (or mayonnaise)	½ cup	125 mL
Grated light medium Cheddar cheese	½ cup	125 mL
Margarine	⅓ cup	75 mL
Hamburger buns, split	8	8

Melt first amount of margarine in frying pan. Add water and onion. Cover. Simmer gently, stirring often, until onion is clear and soft and moisture is evaporated.

Put next 7 ingredients into medium bowl. Mix. Add onion. Stir gently.

Spread second amount of margarine on both halves of buns. Spread turkey mixture on bottom halves. Cover with top halves. Wrap each bun in foil. Heat in 350°F (175°C) oven for about 15 minutes until heated through. Cool slightly before unwrapping. Makes 8.

1 bun: 351 Calories; 18.4 g Total Fat; 636 mg Sodium; 17 g Protein; 29 g Carbohydrate; 1 g Dietary Fiber

TUNA BURGERS

A change from the usual hamburger. Quick to assemble.

Can of tuna, drained and flaked	6½ oz.	184 g
Grated light medium Cheddar cheese	1 cup	250 mL
Light salad dressing (or mayonnaise)	3 tbsp.	50 mL
Sweet pickle relish	2 tbsp.	30 mL
Chopped green onion	2 tbsp.	30 mL
Prepared mustard	2 tsp.	10 mL
Onion powder	1 tsp.	5 mL
Margarine	¼ cup	60 mL
Hamburger buns, split	6	6

Combine first 7 ingredients in small bowl.

Spread margarine on both halves of buns. Spread filling on bottom halves. Cover with top halves. Wrap each bun in foil. Cook on barbecue on medium for about 5 minutes per side until heated through. Cool slightly before unwrapping. Makes 6.

1 burger: 330 Calories; 17.2 g Total Fat; 667 mg Sodium; 16 g Protein; 27 g Carbohydrate; 1 g Dietary Fiber

When margarine is too hard to spread easily, use a vegetable peeler to shave off thin curls. Almost instantly they will be soft and easy to spread.

PORK BUNS

Easy to double. Wrapped buns may be made ahead and chilled until ready to serve.

Boneless pork roast	2½ lbs.	1.1 kg
Water, to almost cover		
Water	½ cup	125 mL
Chicken bouillon powder	1½ tsp.	7 mL
Chopped onion	½ cup	125 mL
Ketchup	½ cup	125 mL
Apple cider vinegar	2½ tbsp.	37 mL
Worcestershire sauce	1½ tsp.	7 mL
Brown sugar, packed	2½ tbsp.	37 mL
Salt	1 tsp.	5 mL
Pepper	¼ tsp.	1 mL
Celery salt	⅛ tsp.	0.5 mL
Chili powder	½ tsp.	2 mL
Margarine	⅔ cup	150 mL
Kaiser rolls (or hamburger buns), split	16	16

Place roast and water in large pot or Dutch oven. Cover. Bring to a boil. Simmer for about 2 hours until pork is tender and pulls apart easily. Remove roast. Shred with fork, discarding fat. Cut shreds into pieces.

Combine water, bouillon powder and onion in small saucepan. Cover. Simmer until onion is soft.

Add next 8 ingredients. Stir. Bring to a boil. Stir in pork pieces.

Spread margarine on both halves of rolls. Spread scant ¼ cup (60 mL) pork mixture on bottom halves. Cover with top halves. Wrap each roll in foil. Heat in 350°F (175°C) oven for 15 minutes until heated through. Cool slightly before unwrapping. Makes 16.

1 bun: 303 Calories; 11.3 g Total Fat; 796 mg Sodium; 15 g Protein; 35 g Carbohydrate; 1 g Dietary Fiber

HAM AND CHEDDAR BUNS

Another all-time favorite.

Can of ham flakes, drained	6½ oz.	184 g
Grated light Cheddar cheese	¾ cup	175 mL
Sweet pickle relish	2 tbsp.	30 mL
Finely chopped onion	1 tbsp.	15 mL
Light salad dressing (or mayonnaise)	2 tbsp.	30 mL
Prepared mustard	1 tsp.	5 mL
Hamburger buns, split	6	6

Mix first 6 ingredients in small bowl. Makes about 1½ cups (375 mL) filling.

Spread over bottom halves of buns. Cover with top halves. Wrap each bun in foil. Heat in 350°F (175°C) oven for about 20 minutes until heated through. Cool slightly before unwrapping. Makes 6.

1 bun: 273 Calories; 12.6 g Total Fat; 814 mg Sodium; 12 g Protein; 26 g Carbohydrate; 1 g Dietary Fiber

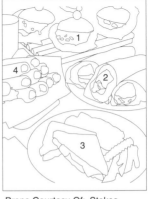

1. BBQ Chicken Buns, page 32
2. Toasty Tuna Torpedoes, page 31
3. Lasagne Sandwich, page 111
4. Corn Doggies, page 98

Props Courtesy Of: Stokes
The Bay

BARBECUE BEEFWICHES

A fast lunch that's ready in ten minutes. Doubles or triples easily.

Barbecue sauce	¼ cup	60 mL
Salsa (mild, medium or hot)	¼ cup	60 mL
Thinly sliced cooked lean beef, cut into strips	½ lb.	225 g
Hamburger buns, split	2	2
Bread and butter pickles, for garnish		

Heat barbecue sauce and salsa in non-stick frying pan. Add beef strips. Mix well to coat. Heat gently until hot.

Toast cut surfaces of buns. Cover with beef mixture. Arrange pickles on beef. Top with top halves. Wrap each bun in foil. Heat in 350°F (175°C) oven for 10 minutes. Cool slightly before unwrapping. Makes 2.

1 sandwich: 363 Calories; 9.1 g Total Fat; 640 mg Sodium; 37 g Protein; 31 g Carbohydrate; 3 g Dietary Fiber

BEAN BURGERS

Make ahead and freeze the uncooked burgers after wrapping in foil.

Can of beans in tomato sauce	14 oz.	398 mL
Ketchup	1 tbsp.	15 mL
Prepared mustard	1 tsp.	5 mL
Finely chopped onion	¼ cup	60 mL
Brown sugar, packed	1 tsp.	5 mL
Grated light Cheddar cheese	½ cup	125 mL
Hamburger buns, split	4	4

Combine first 6 ingredients in small bowl. Mix.

Divide bean mixture evenly on bottom halves of buns. Cover with top halves. Wrap each bun tightly in foil. Bake in 350°F (175°C) oven for 20 minutes until hot and cheese is melted. Cool slightly before unwrapping. If cooking from frozen state, bake for 35 minutes. Makes 4.

1 burger: 293 Calories; 6.1 g Total Fat; 818 mg Sodium; 13 g Protein; 49 g Carbohydrate; 9 g Dietary Fiber

1. Toast Casimir, page 46
2. Sauced Clubhouse Sandwiches, page 43
3. Chicken Zucchini Sandwiches, page 44

Props Courtesy Of: Stokes
The Bay
X/S Wares

Layered Sandwiches

Stack it high or serve it long! These tempting sandwiches are fun to prepare and certain to satisfy the hungriest appetite. The next time you're deciding what to serve for dinner try a classic Clubhouse Sandwich, page 39, or Monte Cristo, page 40.

SANDWICH LOAF

A gorgeous ribbon loaf frosted with cream cheese. Serve with a fork.

Day-old unsliced sandwich bread loaf (use whole wheat, white or both)	1	1
Margarine	½ cup	125 mL
Egg Filling, page 63	1 cup	250 mL
Ham Filling, page 63	1 cup	250 mL
Salmon Filling, page 66	1 cup	250 mL
FROSTING		
Light cream cheese, softened	12 oz.	375 g
Milk	3-4 tbsp.	50-60 mL
Icing (confectioner's) sugar	1 tbsp.	15 mL
Chopped fresh parsley (or chopped nuts), for garnish		

Cut crusts from loaf. Cut lengthwise into 4 even slices.

Lay 1 slice on platter or tray. Spread with margarine. Spread with Egg Filling. Spread second slice with margarine. Place, buttered side down, on top of first filling. Spread top side with margarine. Spread with Ham Filling. Spread third slice with margarine. Place, buttered side down, on top of second filling. Spread top side with margarine. Spread with Salmon Filling. Spread fourth slice with margarine. Place, buttered side down, on top of third filling. Wrap firmly in plastic wrap or foil. Chill for at least 1 hour.

Frosting: Beat cream cheese, milk and icing sugar in medium bowl until good spreading consistency. Frost loaf on top and sides. Decorate with parsley. Chill. Cuts into 12 thick slices.

1 slice: 367 Calories; 23.9 g Total Fat; 1211 mg Sodium; 16 g Protein; 22 g Carbohydrate; 1 g Dietary Fiber

Pictured on page 18.

CLUBHOUSE SANDWICH

A different twist on an old favorite.

Light salad dressing (or mayonnaise)	**1 tbsp.**	**15 mL**
Prepared mustard	**¼ tsp.**	**1 mL**
Margarine	**1 tbsp.**	**15 mL**
White (or whole wheat) bread slices, toasted	**3**	**3**
Cooked chicken slices	**2**	**2**
Salt, sprinkle		
Pepper, sprinkle		
Bacon slices, cooked crisp	**2**	**2**
Lettuce leaf	**1**	**1**
Medium tomato slices	**3**	**3**
Salt, sprinkle		
Pepper, sprinkle		
Very thin slice red onion	**1**	**1**
Thin slice Swiss (or Monterey Jack) cheese	**1**	**1**
Process light Cheddar cheese slice	**1**	**1**
Thin slices dill pickle, for garnish	**4**	**4**

Stir salad dressing and mustard in small bowl.

Spread margarine on 1 side of each toast slice. Layer chicken, salt, pepper, bacon and lettuce on buttered side of first slice. Spread unbuttered side of second slice with ½ of mustard mixture. Place, mustard side down, over lettuce.

Layer tomato, salt, pepper, red onion, and both cheese slices on buttered side of second slice of toast. Spread remaining mustard mixture on buttered side of third slice. Place, mustard side down, over cheese.

Before cutting, push wooden pick down through each quarter. Cut into quarters. Press pickle slice over each wooden pick. Serve as is or heat in microwave on high (100%) for 10 to 20 seconds until cheese is melted a little. Makes 1.

1 sandwich: 701 Calories; 37 g Total Fat; 1154 mg Sodium; 42 g Protein; 49 g Carbohydrate; 2 g Dietary Fiber

Pictured on page 72.

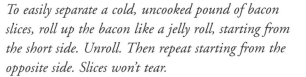

To easily separate a cold, uncooked pound of bacon slices, roll up the bacon like a jelly roll, starting from the short side. Unroll. Then repeat starting from the opposite side. Slices won't tear.

SANDWICH ROLL

Looks alone will make your mouth water.

Margarine	1 tbsp.	15 mL
White (or whole wheat) bread slices, toasted	3	3
Cranberry sauce	1 tbsp.	15 mL
Thin cooked turkey roll slices	3	3
Salt, sprinkle		
Pepper, sprinkle		
Margarine	1 tsp.	5 mL
Medium tomato slices	3	3
Salt, sprinkle		
Pepper, sprinkle		
Lettuce leaf	1	1
Light salad dressing (or mayonnaise)	1-2 tsp.	5-10 mL
Pimiento-stuffed olives (or dill pickle slices), for garnish	2	2

Spread first amount of margarine on 1 side of toast slices. Spread cranberry sauce on 1 slice. Roll up each turkey slice. Place side by side on cranberry sauce. Sprinkle with salt and pepper. Place second toast slice over turkey. Spread second amount of margarine on top side of toast.

Cover with tomato slices, cutting to fit. Sprinkle with salt and pepper. Fold lettuce leaf to fit over tomato. Spread salad dressing on buttered side of third toast slice. Place over lettuce.

Garnish with olives. Cut in half. Makes 1.

1 sandwich: 538 Calories; 25.5 g Total Fat; 1095 mg Sodium; 24 g Protein; 53 g Carbohydrate; 2 g Dietary Fiber

MONTE CRISTO

A sandwich of popular fillings, dipped into egg and grilled.

Margarine	1 tbsp.	15 mL
White (or whole wheat) bread slices	3	3
Part-skim mozzarella cheese slices	2	2
Cooked ham slice	1	1
Turkey (or chicken) slice	1	1
Large egg, fork-beaten	1	1
Water	2 tbsp.	30 mL

Spread margarine on 1 side of bread slices. Layer first bread slice with 1 slice cheese, then ham slice. Top with second bread slice, unbuttered. Layer turkey slice then remaining cheese slice on top. Cover with third bread slice.

Mix egg and water in shallow dish. Dip sandwich into egg mixture. Fry in well-greased frying pan, turning to brown both sides. Cut diagonally into 4. Makes 1.

1 sandwich: 592 Calories; 28 g Total Fat; 1366 mg Sodium; 38 g Protein; 45 g Carbohydrate; 2 g Dietary Fiber

Open-Faced Sandwiches

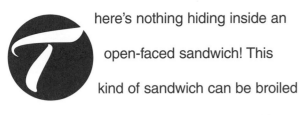

here's nothing hiding inside an open-faced sandwich! This kind of sandwich can be broiled or toasted in the oven and served hot with a gravy or sauce poured over top. Although a little different in presentation than a traditional sandwich, all of these wonderful recipes feature one sure thing—they are certain to appeal to the hungriest of souls at your table.

TOMATO MOZZA ROUNDS

A kid's type bruschetta (pronounced broo-SKET-ah).

Medium tomato, chopped	1	1
Olive oil	1 tbsp.	15 mL
Garlic powder	$\frac{1}{8}$ tsp.	0.5 mL
Salt	$\frac{1}{4}$ tsp.	1 mL
Grated Parmesan cheese	2 tsp.	10 mL
Dried sweet basil	1 tsp.	5 mL
French bread slices (1 inch, 2.5 cm, thick)	2	2
Grated part-skim mozzarella cheese	$\frac{1}{4}$ cup	60 mL
Pitted ripe olives, sliced (optional)	2	2

Combine first 6 ingredients in small bowl. Mix well.

Place bread slices on ungreased baking sheet. Broil on top rack in oven until browned. Turn bread over. Spoon tomato mixture on untoasted side of bread.

Sprinkle with mozzarella cheese and olives. Broil for 2 minutes until cheese is melted. Let stand for 1 minute. Makes 2 large rounds.

1 round: 270 Calories; 11.7 g Total Fat; 746 mg Sodium; 10 g Protein; 32 g Carbohydrate; 2 g Dietary Fiber

Pictured on page 53 and back cover.

STROGANOFF BUNS

A scrumptious layer of chicken stroganoff layered with lettuce, tomato and cheese. Good for lunch— or a sports party.

Cooking oil	2 tbsp.	30 mL
Finely chopped onion	1 cup	250 mL
Lean ground chicken	1¼ lbs.	560 g
All-purpose flour	⅓ cup	75 mL
Beef bouillon powder	2 tsp.	10 mL
Salt	¾ tsp.	4 mL
Pepper	¼ tsp.	1 mL
Water	1¼ cups	300 mL
Can of sliced mushrooms, drained	10 oz.	284 mL
Worcestershire sauce	¼ tsp.	1 mL
Non-fat sour cream	½ cup	125 mL
Margarine	⅓ cup	75 mL
Hamburger buns, split and toasted	7	7
Shredded lettuce, lightly packed	1 cup	250 mL
Thin medium tomato slices	14	14
Grated light Cheddar cheese	⅔ cup	150 mL

Heat cooking oil in frying pan. Add onion and ground chicken. Scramble-fry until no pink remains in chicken and onion is soft.

Mix in flour, bouillon powder, salt and pepper. Stir in water until mixture is boiling and thickened.

Add mushrooms, Worcestershire sauce and sour cream. Heat through without boiling.

Spread margarine on both halves of buns. Arrange 2 halves on individual plates. Top with chicken stroganoff, lettuce, tomato slice and cheese. Makes 3⅔ cups (900 mL) stroganoff, enough for about 14 bun halves using ¼ cup (60 mL) per bun half. Serves 7.

1 serving: 439 Calories; 21.6 g Total Fat; 1096 mg Sodium; 26 g Protein; 35 g Carbohydrate; 3 g Dietary Fiber

TUNA PUFFS

A golden puff with tomato hidden.

Can of tuna, drained and flaked	6½ oz.	184 g
Finely chopped celery	¼ cup	60 mL
Onion powder	⅛ tsp.	0.5 mL
Salt	⅛ tsp.	0.5 mL
Light salad dressing (or mayonnaise)	¼ cup	60 mL
Margarine	2 tbsp.	30 mL
Hamburger buns, split	3	3
Tomato slices	6	6
Light salad dressing (or mayonnaise)	½ cup	125 mL
Grated light Cheddar cheese	¼ cup	60 mL

Mix first 5 ingredients in small bowl.

Spread margarine on both halves of buns. Divide and spread filling on each half.

Lay tomato slice over filling.

Combine second amount of salad dressing and cheese in small bowl. Spread carefully over tomato slices. Broil about 4 inches (10 cm) from heat until puffed and golden. Makes 6 bun halves.

1 bun half: 245 Calories; 14.7 g Total Fat; 602 mg Sodium; 10 g Protein; 18 g Carbohydrate; 1 g Dietary Fiber

SHRIMP BUNS

These can be served immediately or chilled in foil until needed. Simply heat foil-wrapped buns in the oven.

Small or medium cooked shrimp (or 1 can, 4 oz., 113 g, drained and rinsed)	¾ cup	175 mL
Grated light Cheddar cheese	⅓ cup	75 mL
Chopped celery	⅓ cup	75 mL
Onion flakes	2 tsp.	10 mL
Light salad dressing (or mayonnaise)	⅓ cup	75 mL
Parsley flakes	½ tsp.	2 mL
Margarine	2½ tbsp.	37 mL
Hamburger buns, split	4	4

Combine first 6 ingredients in medium bowl. Makes 1 cup (250 mL) filling.

Spread margarine on both halves of buns. Spread filling on each. Arrange on broiler tray. Broil until cheese melts. Makes 8 bun halves.

1 bun half: 161 Calories; 8.7 g Total Fat; 298 mg Sodium; 6 g Protein; 14 g Carbohydrate; 1 g Dietary Fiber

OVEN SHRIMP BUNS: Spread filling on bottom halves of buns. Cover with top halves. Wrap each bun in foil. Chill until needed. Bake in 350°F (175°C) oven for 15 minutes until hot and cheese is melted. Makes 4.

SAUCED CLUBHOUSE SANDWICHES

The open-faced version of the popular layered sandwich. Lots of hot cheese sauce ladled over top.

Margarine	¼ cup	60 mL
White (or whole wheat) bread slices, toasted	12	12
Bacon slices, cooked crisp	12	12
Cooked turkey (or chicken) slices	6	6
Medium tomato slices	12	12
Condensed cheese soup	10 oz.	284 mL
Non-fat sour cream	½ cup	125 mL
Sherry (or alcohol-free sherry)	2 tsp.	10 mL

Spread margarine on each toast slice. Layer bacon, turkey and tomato on 6 toast slices on individual plates.

Heat soup, sour cream and sherry in medium saucepan, stirring occasionally, until boiling. Spoon over top. Arrange remaining 6 toast slices on edge of plates. Makes 6.

1 sandwich: 415 Calories; 21.9 g Total Fat; 1003 mg Sodium; 19 g Protein; 35 g Carbohydrate; 1 g Dietary Fiber

Pictured on page 36.

CHICKEN ZUCCHINI SANDWICHES

Roasted red pepper sauce flows over this attractive luncheon sandwich.

Large boneless, skinless chicken breast halves (see Note)	4	4
Water, to cover		
Salt	½ tsp.	2 mL
PEPPER SAUCE		
Medium red peppers, roasted and peeled	2	2
Margarine	2 tbsp.	30 mL
All-purpose flour	2 tbsp.	30 mL
Salt	¼ tsp.	1 mL
Pepper	⅛ tsp.	0.5 mL
Cayenne pepper	⅛ tsp.	0.5 mL
Milk	1¼ cups	300 mL
Margarine	2 tsp.	10 mL
Medium zucchini, with peel, cut into thin fingers	2	2
Margarine	2½ tbsp.	37 mL
White (or whole wheat) bread slices, toasted	8	8

Place chicken in single layer in medium frying pan. Add water and salt. Cover. Cook until tender. Drain. Cool to handle. Shred chicken. Cover to keep warm.

Pepper Sauce: Cut red peppers in half lengthwise. Remove seeds. Broil, skin side up, for about 10 minutes until charred black. Turn and broil for about 10 minutes until edges are charred black. Peel off skin and discard. Cut up red pepper pieces.

Melt first amount of margarine in small saucepan. Mix in flour, salt, pepper and cayenne pepper. Stir in milk. Heat until mixture is boiling and thickened. Remove from heat. Add red pepper. Process in blender until smooth. Return to saucepan. Cover to keep warm.

Melt second amount of margarine in medium frying pan. Add zucchini. Sauté for about 5 minutes.

Spread third amount of margarine on each toast slice. Cut 4 toast slices in half. Arrange 1 whole and 2 half slices of toast on each plate. Cut each chicken breast half into 2 layers. Arrange 2 pieces of chicken over each center slice of toast. Spoon red pepper sauce over chicken. Spoon zucchini over top. Makes 4.

1 sandwich: 484 Calories; 19.2 g Total Fat; 760 mg Sodium; 37 g Protein; 40 g Carbohydrate; 3 g Dietary Fiber

Pictured on page 36.

Note: If chicken breasts aren't large, cook 1 extra to fill space on toast.

Keep a pair of wooden chopsticks near the toaster to safely remove bread slices that have become stuck inside.

Loaf O' Plenty

A centerpiece that tastes as good as it looks.

French bread loaf	1	1
Margarine	¼ cup	60 mL
Light salad dressing (or mayonnaise)	⅓ cup	75 mL
Prepared mustard	2 tbsp.	30 mL
Part-skim mozzarella cheese slices	4	4
Swiss cheese slices	4	4
Cooked ham slices	4	4
Salami slices	4	4
Pimiento loaf slices	4	4
Macaroni loaf slices	4	4
Green, red or yellow pepper rings	8	8
Curly lettuce leaves	8	8

Cut loaf to bottom but not through, into 16 slices. Spread both sides of slices, except outer ends, with margarine, salad dressing and mustard.

Insert 1 cheese slice, 2 meat slices, 1 pepper ring and lettuce into each section. Place on cutting board. Cut through bottom crust to serve. Makes 8.

1 sandwich: 417 Calories; 21.2 g Total Fat; 1311 mg Sodium; 19 g Protein; 36 g Carbohydrate; 1 g Dietary Fiber

MINI MUNCH: Cut individual Italian loaf into 4 slices, cutting to but not through bottom. Spread margarine, salad dressing and mustard on all cut sides as desired. Insert above fillings as desired. Wrap in plastic wrap or waxed paper for a great hold-in-both-hands sandwich. Makes 1.

Pictured on page 54.

Loaf Of Pizza

Topping can be ready ahead of time for a quick last minute snack.

French bread loaf	1	1
Lean ground beef	1 lb.	454 g
Tomato sauce	7½ oz.	213 mL
Ground oregano	½ tsp.	2 mL
Dried sweet basil	½ tsp.	2 mL
Beef bouillon powder	½ tsp.	2 mL
Salt	¼ tsp.	1 mL
Pepper	¼ tsp.	1 mL
Onion powder	¼ tsp.	1 mL
Green onions, chopped	2	2
Sweet pickle relish	2 tbsp.	30 mL
Granulated sugar	½ tsp.	2 mL
Grated medium Cheddar cheese	1 cup	250 mL
Medium tomatoes, thinly sliced	2	2
Grated part-skim mozzarella cheese	1 cup	250 mL
Grated Parmesan cheese	2 tbsp.	30 mL

Slice loaf lengthwise into 2 halves. Arrange on ungreased baking sheet.

Scramble-fry ground beef in large non-stick frying pan until no longer pink. Drain well.

Add next 10 ingredients to beef. Stir. Spread over bread halves.

Sprinkle remaining 4 ingredients over beef mixture in order given. Bake on bottom rack in 350°F (175°C) oven for about 20 minutes. Cuts into 6 thick slices each, making 12 slices in total.

1 slice: 251 Calories; 9.6 g Total Fat; 568 mg Sodium; 16 g Protein; 25 g Carbohydrate; 1 g Dietary Fiber

TOAST CASIMIR

Banana, currants and chicken—very unusual. Mild curry flavor. Excellent choice.

Margarine	2½ tbsp.	37 mL
All-purpose flour	2½ tbsp.	37 mL
Salt	½ tsp.	2 mL
Pepper	¼ tsp.	1 mL
Curry powder	¾ tsp.	4 mL
Milk	3 cups	750 mL
Light salad dressing (or mayonnaise)	¾ cup	175 mL
Slivered red pepper	¼ cup	60 mL
Currants (or cut up raisins)	3 tbsp.	50 mL
Green-tipped medium bananas, halved lengthwise and sliced	1½	1½
Chopped cooked chicken (or turkey)	3 cups	750 mL
White (or whole wheat) bread slices, toasted	8	8

Melt first amount of margarine in large saucepan. Mix in flour, salt, pepper and curry powder. Stir in milk until mixture is boiling and thickened.

Add salad dressing. Stir. Add next 4 ingredients. Stir to heat through.

Place 1 toast slice on each of 2 salad or luncheon plates. Cut other 4 slices in half diagonally. Place 2 halves on each plate, 1 on each side of whole slice. Spoon chicken mixture over center slice. Makes 4.

1 sandwich: 684 Calories; 26.9 g Total Fat; 1245 mg Sodium; 47 g Protein; 62 g Carbohydrate; 2 g Dietary Fiber

Pictured on page 36.

PIZZA MUFFINS

Kids of all ages choose these first. So easy.

Margarine	1 tsp.	5 mL
Lean ground beef	1 lb.	454 g
Chopped onion	½ cup	125 mL
Salt	1 tsp.	5 mL
Tomato paste	5½ oz.	156 mL
Worcestershire sauce	1 tsp.	5 mL
Italian seasoning	1 tsp.	5 mL
Margarine	2 tbsp.	30 mL
English muffins, split	6	6
Part-skim mozzarella cheese slices	6	6
Grated Parmesan cheese	2 tbsp.	30 mL
Chopped green onion	¼ cup	60 mL

Melt first amount of margarine in frying pan. Add ground beef, onion and salt. Scramble-fry slowly until no pink remains in beef and onion is soft.

Add tomato paste, Worcestershire sauce and Italian seasoning. Stir.

Spread second amount of margarine on both halves of muffins. Spread beef mixture over muffin halves. Cut cheese slices in half. Put ½ of slice over beef mixture. Sprinkle with Parmesan cheese. Top with green onion. Broil. Makes 12.

1 muffin half: 218 Calories; 10.6 g Total Fat; 474 mg Sodium; 13 g Protein; 18 g Carbohydrate; 1 g Dietary Fiber

CHICKEN MELT

A colorful open-faced sandwich. A warm tomato slice tops the cheese.

Margarine	1 tsp.	5 mL
White (or whole wheat) bread slice, toasted	1	1
Cooked chicken slices	2-3	2-3
Coleslaw (or drained sauerkraut)	⅓ cup	75 mL
Process light Cheddar (or Swiss or mozzarella) cheese slices	2	2
Medium tomato slice, warmed in oven, microwave or frying pan	1	1
Dried sweet basil, just a pinch		
Gherkin (or small dill pickle), halved lengthwise	1	1

Spread margarine on toast slice. Lay slice on broiler tray. Layer with chicken, coleslaw and cheese. Broil to melt cheese.

Transfer to plate. Lay tomato slice on top. Sprinkle with basil.

Overlap gherkin halves on the side. Makes 1.

1 sandwich: 380 Calories; 16.4 g Total Fat; 616 mg Sodium; 32 g Protein; 24 g Carbohydrate; 1 g Dietary Fiber

PITA PIZZA

If you like a thin-crust pizza this is the one for you.

Pita bread (8 inch, 20 cm, size)	1	1
Commercial pizza (or spaghetti) sauce	2 tbsp.	30 mL
Chopped cooked ham (or pepperoni, bacon or sausage)	2 tbsp.	30 mL
Fresh mushrooms, chopped	2	2
Grated part-skim mozzarella cheese	⅓ cup	75 mL
Diced green pepper	2 tbsp.	30 mL

Place pita bread on ungreased baking sheet. Flatten with your hand.

Spread pizza sauce over pita almost to edges.

Sprinkle ham, mushrooms, cheese and green pepper over sauce. Broil on top rack in oven for about 7 minutes until cheese is melted and edge of pita is crisp. Cuts into 6 wedges.

1 wedge: 60 Calories; 1.5 g Total Fat; 150 mg Sodium; 4 g Protein; 8 g Carbohydrate; trace Dietary Fiber

HAM AND EGGS PIZZA

Tomato sauce is good in this but for a different taste, try it with jalapeño jelly. A full meal deal.

Basic Pizza Crust dough, page 13	1	1
Margarine	1 tbsp.	15 mL
Large eggs	12	12
Water	1/3 cup	75 mL
Salt	1 tsp.	5 mL
Pepper	1/4 tsp.	1 mL
Commercial pizza sauce	1/2 cup	125 mL
Cooked ham (at least 1/8 inch, 3 mm, thick), cut into 1/2 x 1 inch (12 mm x 2.5 cm) pieces	10 oz.	285 g
Grated Edam cheese	3/4 cup	175 mL
Grated part-skim mozzarella cheese	3/4 cup	175 mL

Prepare pizza dough. Roll out and press in greased 12 inch (30 cm) pizza pan, forming rim around edge.

Melt margarine in large frying pan. Beat next 4 ingredients in medium bowl. Pour into frying pan. Scramble-fry until egg is cooked. Do not overcook.

Spread crust with pizza sauce. Spoon scrambled eggs over top.

Top with ham. Toss both cheeses together in small bowl. Layer over ham. Bake on bottom rack in 425°F (220°C) oven for 13 to 15 minutes, or for about 8 minutes if using partially baked crust. Cuts into 8 wedges.

1 wedge: 397 Calories; 20.1 g Total Fat; 1092 mg Sodium; 23 g Protein; 30 g Carbohydrate; 1 g Dietary Fiber

CHEESE PUFFS

Cutting these in half exposes a colorful layer of asparagus, cheese and tomato.

Margarine	2 tsp.	10 mL
White (or whole wheat) bread slices, toasted	2	2
Medium tomato slices	4	4
Process light Cheddar cheese slices	2	2
Canned asparagus spears (or fresh, cooked)	8	8
Egg white (large)	1	1
Egg yolk (large)	1	1
Low-fat French dressing	1 tsp.	5 mL
Salt, sprinkle		
Pepper, sprinkle		

Spread margarine on 1 side of toast slices. Layer tomato, cheese and asparagus on slices.

Beat egg white in medium bowl until stiff.

Mix egg yolk, dressing, salt and pepper in small bowl. Fold into egg white. Spread over asparagus. Bake in 350°F (175°C) oven for about 15 minutes until light brown. Cut in half to serve. Makes 2.

1 sandwich: 234 Calories; 12 g Total Fat; 417 mg Sodium; 13 g Protein; 19 g Carbohydrate; 2 g Dietary Fiber

Pictured on page 18.

SPEEDY PIZZA

French bread, cut into layers, makes an ideal instant crust. Good snack food.

French bread loaf	1	1
Margarine	3 tbsp.	50 mL
Chopped onion	1 cup	250 mL
Cooking oil	2 tsp.	10 mL
Tomato sauce	7½ oz.	213 mL
Dried whole oregano	½ tsp.	2 mL
Dried sweet basil	½ tsp.	2 mL
Garlic powder	¼ tsp.	1 mL
Salt	¼ tsp.	1 mL
Pepper	⅛ tsp.	0.5 mL
Chopped salami, summer sausage or pepperoni (or all three)	1½ cups	375 mL
Grated Parmesan cheese	¼ cup	60 mL
Part-skim mozzarella cheese slices	6	6

Slice loaf lengthwise into 2 halves. Spread margarine on cut sides. Place on ungreased baking sheet, cut side up.

Sauté onion in cooking oil in medium frying pan until soft.

Stir next 6 ingredients in small bowl. Spread over loaf halves. Divide onion over each.

Scatter meat over each. Sprinkle with Parmesan cheese. Arrange mozzarella cheese slices over top. Bake on bottom rack in 350°F (175°C) oven for about 20 minutes. Each half cuts into 6 thick slices, for a total of 12.

1 slice: 259 Calories; 13 g Total Fat; 725 mg Sodium; 11 g Protein; 25 g Carbohydrate; 1 g Dietary Fiber

REUBEN PIZZA

If you like Reuben sandwiches, this is for you. You might choose to use the whole jar of sauerkraut.

Rye Pizza Crust dough, page 15	1	1
THOUSAND ISLAND SAUCE		
Salad dressing (or mayonnaise)	⅓ cup	75 mL
Chili sauce	3 tbsp.	50 mL
Sweet pickle relish	1½ tbsp.	25 mL
Minced onion flakes	1 tsp.	5 mL
TOPPING		
Grated Edam (or mozzarella) cheese	¾ cup	175 mL
Jar of sauerkraut, (17½ oz., 500 mL), drained and squeezed dry	½	½
Can of corned beef, sliced and chopped	7 oz.	198 g
Grated part-skim mozzarella cheese	¾ cup	175 mL

Prepare pizza dough. Roll out and press in greased 12 inch (30 cm) pizza pan, forming rim around edge.

Thousand Island Sauce: Mix all 4 ingredients in small bowl. Spread over crust.

Topping: Sprinkle Edam cheese over sauce. Add layer of sauerkraut. Scatter corned beef and mozzarella cheese over top. Bake on bottom rack in 425°F (220°C) oven for 13 to 15 minutes. Cuts into 8 wedges.

1 wedge: 355 Calories; 17.6 g Total Fat; 807 mg Sodium; 16 g Protein; 33 g Carbohydrate; 4 g Dietary Fiber

MEXICAN FLATBREAD PIZZA

As a variation, omit the flatbread and serve in taco shells or wrapped in tortillas.

Minute (or fast-fry) steaks, 1/4 inch (6 mm) thick	1 lb.	454 g
Chunky salsa (mild, medium or hot)	1/2 cup	125 mL
Lime juice	2 tbsp.	30 mL
Flatbread or prebaked pizza crust (12 inch, 30 cm)	1	1
Chunky salsa (mild, medium or hot)	1/2 cup	125 mL
Grated Monterey Jack cheese	1/4 cup	60 mL
Grated medium Cheddar cheese	1/4 cup	60 mL

Marinate steaks in first amount of salsa and lime juice in shallow dish for 15 minutes.

Place flatbread on ungreased baking sheet in warm oven while preparing steaks. Remove steaks, discarding marinade. Cook steaks in frying pan for 2 minutes per side or until desired doneness. Cut into thin strips.

Spread flatbread with second amount of salsa. Top with steak strips. Sprinkle with both cheeses. Broil for 2 minutes until cheese is melted. Cuts into 8 wedges.

1 wedge: 237 Calories; 7.3 g Total Fat; 560 mg Sodium; 18 g Protein; 24 g Carbohydrate; 1 g Dietary Fiber

PITA PIZZAS

Cut into small wedges to serve as an appetizer.

Lean ground beef	1/2 lb.	225 g
Finely diced onion	1/3 cup	75 mL
Ground oregano	1/4 tsp.	1 mL
Salt	1/4 tsp.	1 mL
Garlic powder	1/4 tsp.	1 mL
Whole wheat pita breads (6 inch, 15 cm, size)	8	8
Tomato (or pizza) sauce	7 1/2 oz.	213 mL
Finely chopped fresh mushrooms	1 cup	250 mL
Finely diced green pepper	1 1/2 cups	375 mL
Grated part-skim mozzarella cheese	2 cups	500 mL

Scramble-fry ground beef, onion, oregano, salt and garlic powder in non-stick frying pan until onion is soft and beef is no longer pink. Drain.

Place pita breads on ungreased baking sheet. Flatten, using a rolling pin or your hand. Spread each pita with about 1 1/2 tbsp. (25 mL) tomato sauce. Sprinkle with 3 tbsp. (50 mL) beef mixture, 2 tbsp. (30 mL) mushrooms and 2 tbsp. (30 mL) green pepper. Sprinkle 1/4 cup (60 mL) cheese over top. Broil 6 to 8 inches (15 to 20 cm) from heat until edges are crusty and cheese is melted. Cut into quarters to serve. Makes 8.

1 pizza: 301 Calories; 8 g Total Fat; 544 mg Sodium; 19 g Protein; 39 g Carbohydrate; 5 g Dietary Fiber

HAM BROCCOLI PIZZA

Looks so appealing with its orange-yellow topping with bits of broccoli and ham showing through.

Basic Pizza Crust, page 13	1	1
Broccoli florets Boiling water, to cover	2 cups	500 mL
Light cream cheese, softened	4 oz.	125 g
Prepared mustard	2 tbsp.	30 mL
Prepared horseradish	1 tsp.	5 mL
Cooked ham, 1/4 inch (6 mm) thick, cut into 1/2 inch (12 mm) pieces (or smaller)	1/2 lb.	225 g
Chopped green onion	2 tbsp.	30 mL
Grated medium Cheddar cheese	3/4 cup	175 mL
Grated part-skim mozzarella cheese	3/4 cup	175 mL

Prepare pizza dough. Roll out and press in greased 12 inch (30 cm) pizza pan, forming rim around edge.

Cook broccoli in boiling water in medium saucepan until tender-crisp. Do not overcook. Drain.

Mash cream cheese, mustard and horseradish together in small bowl until smooth. Spread over crust. Scatter broccoli over top.

Top with ham and green onion.

Toss Cheddar cheese and mozzarella cheese together in small bowl. Sprinkle over top. Bake on bottom rack in 425°F (220°C) oven for 13 to 15 minutes, or for about 8 minutes if using partially baked crust. Let stand for 5 to 10 minutes before cutting to allow cream cheese to firm up a bit. Cuts into 8 wedges.

1 wedge: 321 Calories; 15.2 g Total Fat; 786 mg Sodium; 17 g Protein; 29 g Carbohydrate; 2 g Dietary Fiber

SALSA PIZZA

Salsa instead of pizza sauce—zippy!

Pita bread (6 inch, 15 cm, size)	1	1
Chunky salsa (mild, medium or hot)	2 tbsp.	30 mL
Grated light Cheddar (or part-skim mozzarella) cheese	1/3 cup	75 mL
Diced green or red pepper (optional)	1/4 cup	60 mL

Place pita bread on ungreased baking sheet. Flatten with your hand.

Spread salsa on pita bread. Sprinkle with cheese. Add green pepper. Bake in 400°F (205°C) oven for about 10 minutes until cheese is melted and edge of pita is crisp. Let stand for 2 minutes before cutting. Cuts into 6 wedges.

1 wedge: 50 Calories; 1.5 g Total Fat; 154 mg Sodium; 3 g Protein; 6 g Carbohydrate; trace Dietary Fiber

MINI PIZZAS

Great when served immediately or cooked from the frozen state.

Tomato paste	5½ oz.	156 mL
Garlic powder	⅛ tsp.	0.5 mL
Onion powder	½ tsp.	2 mL
Dried whole oregano	¼ tsp.	1 mL
Dried sweet basil	¼ tsp.	1 mL
Olive oil	1 tbsp.	15 mL
Finely chopped cooked ham (or pepperoni, bacon or sausage)	½ cup	125 mL
Finely chopped green pepper (optional)	¼ cup	60 mL
Finely chopped fresh mushrooms (optional)	¼ cup	60 mL
English muffins (or hamburger buns), split	5	5
Grated part-skim mozzarella cheese	1 cup	250 mL

Combine first 6 ingredients in medium bowl. Stir to mix well.

Add ham, green pepper and mushrooms. Divide mixture on each muffin half. Place on ungreased baking sheet.

Sprinkle with mozzarella cheese. Bake in 350°F (175°C) oven for 10 minutes until cheese is melted. (These can be wrapped airtight before baking and then frozen to be cooked as needed at 400°F, 205°C, for 15 minutes.) Makes 10.

1 pizza: 142 Calories; 4.7 g Total Fat; 283 mg Sodium; 8 g Protein; 17 g Carbohydrate; 1 g Dietary Fiber

CORNED BEEF BUNS

Spoon this cheesy spread on buns and bake for a delicious snack.

Pasteurized cheese loaf, cut up	4 oz.	125 g
Margarine	2 tbsp.	30 mL
Prepared mustard	1 tsp.	5 mL
Onion powder	¼ tsp.	1 mL
Can of corned beef, chopped	12 oz.	340 g
Hamburger buns, split	2	2

Put cheese, margarine, mustard and onion powder into medium saucepan. Heat over low, stirring frequently, until melted and smooth.

Add corned beef. Stir. Makes about 1½ cups (375 mL).

Spread on bun halves. Bake in 400°F (205°C) oven for 10 to 15 minutes. Makes 4.

1 bun half: 436 Calories; 27.6 g Total Fat; 1555 mg Sodium; 31 g Protein; 14 g Carbohydrate; 1 g Dietary Fiber

1. Beef Dip Sandwiches, page 22
2. Tomato Mozza Rounds, page 41
3. Asparagus Ham Rolls, page 59

Props Courtesy Of: Pacific Linen
Stokes
The Bay

ONION MELT

If you have never had cheese and onion together, you are in for a treat. Top with two slices of cheese for more of a treat yet.

Sliced onion	1⅓ cups	325 mL
Cold water, to cover		
Boiling water, to cover		
White (or whole wheat) bread slices, toasted	4	4
Part-skim mozzarella cheese slices	4	4
Paprika, sprinkle		

Soak onion in cold water in small bowl for 30 minutes. Drain.

Put onion into small saucepan. Add boiling water. Cover. Simmer until soft. Drain.

Divide onion on toast slices. Lay cheese slices over top of onion. Sprinkle with paprika. Broil until cheese is melted and browned slightly. Makes 4.

1 melt: 183 Calories; 6.3 g Total Fat; 307 mg Sodium; 12 g Protein; 20 g Carbohydrate; 1 g Dietary Fiber

MUSHROOM TRIANGLES

Try the filling, broiled, on open-faced buns as well as on these tasty triangles.

Sliced fresh mushrooms	1½ cups	375 mL
Chopped onion	¼ cup	60 mL
Margarine, melted	1 tsp.	5 mL
Light cream cheese, cut up	4 oz.	125 g
Worcestershire sauce	¼ tsp.	1 mL
Salt	¼ tsp.	1 mL
Pepper, sprinkle		
Garlic powder, sprinkle		
White (or whole wheat) bread slices, crusts removed	4	4
Margarine, melted	1 tbsp.	15 mL

Sauté mushrooms and onion in first amount of margarine in frying pan until onion is clear and soft.

Add next 5 ingredients. Stir to melt cream cheese. Makes about ⅔ cup (150 mL) filling.

Divide and spread filling on bread slices. Fold to make triangle. Press edges. Brush top sides with second amount of margarine. Toast triangles in 400°F (205°C) oven for 10 to 15 minutes. Makes 4.

1 triangle: 177 Calories; 9.7 g Total Fat; 642 mg Sodium; 6 g Protein; 17 g Carbohydrate; 1 g Dietary Fiber

Variation: Flatten bread slices slightly with rolling pin. Spread filling to edges. Roll up and secure with wooden picks. Brush with melted margarine. Toast as above.

1. Mini Munch, page 45
2. Cucumber Under Wraps, page 60
3. Ham And Cheese Delights, page 57

Rolled Sandwiches

With these great recipes at your fingertips, you will never worry about serving "the same old sandwich." Rolled sandwiches are neat, very pretty in their presentation and perfect to serve company. But the best thing about rolled sandwiches is that they look so much harder to make than they actually are!

PEANUT BUTTER WRAP

Much more fun than your ordinary peanut butter sandwich.

Peanut butter (smooth or crunchy)	2 tbsp.	30 mL
White (or whole wheat) flour tortilla (10 inch, 25 cm, size), page 16, or commercial	1	1
Chopped apple, with peel	½ cup	125 mL
Brown sugar, packed	1 tsp.	5 mL
Ground cinnamon	¼ tsp.	1 mL

Spread peanut butter on tortilla. Scatter apple over top.

Combine brown sugar and cinnamon in cup. Sprinkle over apple. Roll up tortilla tightly. Wrap with plastic wrap. Chill. Makes 1.

1 wrap: 330 Calories; 9 g Total Fat; 685 mg Sodium; 9 g Protein; 24 g Carbohydrate; 3 g Dietary Fiber

Pictured on page 89.

JAM ROLL-UP

A real treat. Quick after-school snack for the kids.

Margarine	1 tsp.	5 mL
White (or whole wheat) bread slice, crust removed	1	1
Jam (or jelly)	1 tbsp.	15 mL
Liquid honey	1 tbsp.	15 mL

Spread margarine on bread slice.

Mix jam and honey in small bowl. Spread over margarine. Roll up and secure with wooden pick. Toast in 400°F (205°C) oven until golden brown. Makes 1.

1 roll-up: 214 Calories; 4.6 g Total Fat; 168 mg Sodium; 2 g Protein; 43 g Carbohydrate; 1 g Dietary Fiber

HAM AND CHEESE DELIGHTS

Pack one or two of these in your school lunch.
Great warm or cold.

Light cream cheese, softened	8 oz.	250 g
Sweet pickle relish	1½ tbsp.	25 mL
Cooked ham slices, diced	5	5
Onion powder	¼ tsp.	1 mL
Refrigerator crescent-style rolls (8 per tube)	8½ oz.	235 g

Combine cream cheese, relish, ham and onion powder in small bowl. Mix well.

Open crescent roll tube and separate dough into 8 triangles. Spread 2 tbsp. (30 mL) ham mixture on each triangle. Roll up from shortest side of triangle to opposite point. Place rolls on ungreased baking sheet. Bake in 375°F (190°C) oven for 12 minutes until golden brown. Makes 8.

1 roll: 144 Calories; 8.7 g Total Fat; 770 mg Sodium; 8 g Protein; 8 g Carbohydrate; trace Dietary Fiber

Pictured on page 54.

BACON CHEESE ROLL-UP

A new way to serve grilled cheese and bacon.

White (or whole wheat) bread slice, crust removed	1	1
Process cheese spread	1 tbsp.	15 mL
Bacon slices, cooked, but not crisp, cut in half	2	2
Margarine, melted	1 tsp.	5 mL

Flatten bread slice slightly with rolling pin. Spread with process cheese. Lay bacon pieces on cheese. Roll up and secure with wooden pick.

Brush with melted margarine. Toast in 400°F (205°C) oven until golden brown, or broil. Makes 1.

1 roll-up: 468 Calories; 35.3 g Total Fat; 1322 mg Sodium; 22 g Protein; 14 g Carbohydrate; trace Dietary Fiber

Pictured on page 89.

"WURST" CHEESE AND LETTUCE WRAP

Very easy and quick to make. Use more liverwurst if you like.

Plain (or herbed) liverwurst	2 tbsp.	30 mL
White (or whole wheat) flour tortilla (10 inch, 25 cm, size), page 16, or commercial	1	1
Grated Swiss cheese	⅓ cup	75 mL
Shredded lettuce, lightly packed	⅓-½ cup	75-125 mL

Spread liverwurst on tortilla. Sprinkle with cheese and lettuce. Roll up tightly. Wrap with plastic wrap. Chill. Makes 1.

1 wrap: 315 Calories; 25.7 g Total Fat; 813 mg Sodium; 15 g Protein; 6 g Carbohydrate; trace Dietary Fiber

VEGETABLE ROLL

Try different flavored dressings for a variety of tastes.

Spreadable light cream cheese	1 tbsp.	15 mL
Low-fat ranch (or other creamy) dressing	1 tbsp.	15 mL
White (or whole wheat) flour tortilla (10 inch, 25 cm, size), page 16, or commercial	1	1
Grated carrot	2 tbsp.	30 mL
Finely chopped green, red or yellow pepper	2 tbsp.	30 mL
Finely chopped green onion	2 tsp.	10 mL
Finely chopped broccoli florets	3 tbsp.	50 mL
Grated light Cheddar cheese	¼ cup	60 mL

Combine cream cheese and dressing in small bowl. Stir.

Spread on tortilla, almost to edge.

Sprinkle with remaining 5 ingredients in order given. Roll up tightly. Wrap with plastic wrap. Chill. Makes 1.

1 roll: 298 Calories; 23.5 g Total Fat; 651 mg Sodium; 11 g Protein; 11 g Carbohydrate; 1 g Dietary Fiber

Pictured on page 108.

CRAB ROLLS

Whether in toasted bread rolls or heated on buns, the filling is a winner every time.

Light cream cheese, softened	4 oz.	125 g
Can of crabmeat, drained and cartilage removed	5 oz.	142 g
Finely chopped onion	1 tbsp.	15 mL
Prepared horseradish	¼ tsp.	1 mL
Salt	⅛ tsp.	0.5 mL
Ground almonds	2 tbsp.	30 mL
White (or whole wheat) bread slices, crusts removed	8	8

Mash first 6 ingredients together in small bowl. Makes about 1½ cups (375 mL) filling.

Flatten bread slices slightly with rolling pin. Spread filling on bread slices to edges. Roll up and secure with wooden picks. Bake in 400°F (205°C) oven until golden. Makes 8.

1 roll: 122 Calories; 4.4 g Total Fat; 436 mg Sodium; 7 g Protein; 14 g Carbohydrate; 1 g Dietary Fiber

Pictured on page 18.

To roll up a long sandwich loaf slice, place slice on a damp tea towel. Spread the filling on and roll up tightly, using the towel.

LETTUCE ROLLS

These are best made in the morning before school. Lettuce leaves will become soggy if rolls are made the night before. Peel down the plastic wrap as you eat the roll.

Large lettuce leaves	4	4
Cooked ham slices (or other sliced deli meat)	2	2
Prepared mustard	1 tbsp.	15 mL

Lay lettuce leaves on working surface, making 2 stacks of 2 lettuce leaves each. Lay 1 slice of ham over each stack. Spread mustard over ham. Roll up tightly. Wrap with plastic wrap. Chill. Makes 2.

1 roll: 58 Calories; 2.2 g Total Fat; 610 mg Sodium; 8 g Protein; 2 g Carbohydrate; 1 g Dietary Fiber

Variation: Place carrot stick, cheese stick, dill pickle wedge or folded cheese slice on top of ham before rolling. Use salad dressing (or mayonnaise) instead of mustard.

How do you clean a mustard stain? Use a mixture of 5% hydrogen peroxide and a few drops of ammonia. Peroxide and ammonia can both be found in the pharmacy and cleaning sections of the larger grocery stores. Test mixture on an out-of-the-way area of the clothing, then proceed to wash by hand.

ASPARAGUS HAM ROLLS

Hot toasted rolls make a different lunch treat, especially when they can be made ahead and chilled until needed. These brown better if brushed with melted margarine first.

White (or whole wheat) bread slices, crusts removed	12	12
Margarine	¼ cup	60 mL
Cooked ham slices	12	12
Canned asparagus spears (or fresh, cooked)	12	12
Process light Cheddar cheese slices (optional)		

Flatten bread slices slightly with rolling pin. Spread with margarine. Add slice of ham. Put asparagus spear on 1 side. Roll up and secure with wooden picks. May be covered with damp tea towel to hold in refrigerator. To serve, place on greased baking sheet. Brown in 400°F (205°C) oven for about 10 minutes. Makes 12.

1 roll: 154 Calories; 6.6 g Total Fat; 688 mg Sodium; 9 g Protein; 14 g Carbohydrate; 1 g Dietary Fiber

Pictured on page 53 and back cover.

Variation: Use asparagus and cheese only, or ham and a bit of prepared mustard.

ROAST BEEF ROLL

Tastes better if made the night before.

Plain (or herbed) non-fat spreadable cream cheese	3 tbsp.	50 mL
White (or whole wheat) flour tortilla (10 inch, 25 cm, size), page 16, or commercial	1	1
Shredded lettuce, lightly packed	½ cup	125 mL
Finely diced onion	1 tbsp.	15 mL
Shaved roast beef (or 3 very thin slices)	2 oz.	57 g

Spread cream cheese on 1 side of tortilla. Cover with lettuce and onion. Lay beef over top of onion. Roll up tightly and wrap with plastic wrap. Chill for at least 1 hour or overnight. Makes 1.

1 roll: 228 Calories; 11 g Total Fat; 568 mg Sodium; 20 g Protein; 12 g Carbohydrate; 1 g Dietary Fiber

BEEF ROLLS

Warm and cheesy.

Ground cooked roast beef	1 cup	250 mL
Grated light Cheddar cheese	½ cup	125 mL
Light salad dressing (or mayonnaise)	¼ cup	60 mL
Salt	½ tsp.	2 mL
Pepper	⅛ tsp.	0.5 mL
White (or whole wheat) bread slices, crusts removed	4	4

Mix first 5 ingredients in small bowl, adding more salad dressing if too dry. Check seasoning. Makes about 1 cup (250 mL) filling.

Flatten bread slices slightly with rolling pin. Divide and spread filling over each. Roll up and secure with wooden picks. Toast in 400°F (205°C) oven until golden brown. Makes 4.

1 roll: 239 Calories; 10.3 g Total Fat; 714 mg Sodium; 19 g Protein; 15 g Carbohydrate; trace Dietary Fiber

CUCUMBER UNDER WRAPS

Pack these for your lunch. Easy to eat.

Plain (or herbed) non-fat spreadable cream cheese	½ cup	125 mL
White (or whole wheat) flour tortillas (8 inch, 20 cm, size)	4	4
Cucumber piece, 6 inches (15 cm) long, quartered lengthwise	1	1
Salt, sprinkle (optional)		
Pepper, sprinkle (optional)		

Spread 2 tbsp. (30 mL) cream cheese on each tortilla.

Lay 1 cucumber spear across 1 side of each tortilla. Sprinkle with salt and pepper. Roll up each tortilla around cucumber. Wrap tightly with plastic wrap. Chill. Makes 4.

1 roll: 175 Calories; 5.3 g Total Fat; 332 mg Sodium; 5 g Protein; 27 g Carbohydrate; 1 g Dietary Fiber

Pictured on page 54.

Sandwich Fillings

 t's time for lunch, and the peanut butter jar is empty. Well, get ready to find yourself amidst all kinds of alternatives for the family! This section is filled (no pun intended) with some of the tastiest and diverse recipes for sandwich fillings ever. There is something for everyone.

CHICKEN FILLING

Try some variety. Flavorful and crunchy.

Boneless, skinless chicken breast half	1	1
Water, to cover		
Very finely chopped celery	3 tbsp.	50 mL
Lemon juice	½ tsp.	2 mL
Curry powder, just a pinch		
Light salad dressing (or mayonnaise)	⅔ cup	150 mL
Salt	⅛ tsp.	0.5 mL
Toasted almonds, finely chopped	3 tbsp.	50 mL

Cover chicken with water in small saucepan. Cover. Bring to a boil. Simmer until tender. Drain. When cool enough to handle, chop finely. This gives a better texture than grinding.

Combine remaining 6 ingredients in small bowl. Add chicken. Stir well. Makes 1⅔ cups (400 mL).

2 tbsp. (30 mL): 53 Calories; 4 g Total Fat; 124 mg Sodium; 2 g Protein; 2 g Carbohydrate; trace Dietary Fiber

To toast almonds, place in single layer in ungreased shallow baking dish. Bake in 350°F (175°C) oven for 5 to 8 minutes, watching carefully so they don't burn.

CHICKEN CURRY FILLING

The curry flavor is mild.

Finely chopped cooked chicken	2 cups	500 mL
Light salad dressing (or mayonnaise)	¼ cup	60 mL
Non-fat sour cream	2 tbsp.	30 mL
Curry powder	¼ tsp.	1 mL
Salt	½ tsp.	2 mL

Mix all 5 ingredients in small bowl. If you want a softer spread, add a bit of milk. Makes 1½ cups (375 mL).

2 tbsp. (30 mL): 63 Calories; 2.3 g Total Fat; 170 mg Sodium; 9 g Protein; 1 g Carbohydrate; trace Dietary Fiber

Pictured on front cover.

CHICKEN EGG FILLING

A sandwich that contains both the chicken and the egg. This filling does not freeze well.

Finely chopped cooked chicken	2 cups	500 mL
Large hard-boiled egg, chopped	1	1
Chopped green onion	2 tbsp.	30 mL
Light salad dressing (or mayonnaise)	6 tbsp.	100 mL
Salt	½ tsp.	2 mL
Pepper	⅛ tsp.	0.5 mL

Combine all 6 ingredients in small bowl. Mix well. A bit of milk may be added to make a softer spread. Makes 1¾ cups (425 mL).

2 tbsp. (30 mL): 64 Calories; 2.8 g Total Fat; 163 mg Sodium; 8 g Protein; 1 g Carbohydrate; trace Dietary Fiber

CRUNCHY CHICKEN FILLING

Celery is added for crunch. Great to have on hand. Store in refrigerator for up to five days. Freeze, without the celery, for up to three months. Add celery after filling has thawed.

Ground cooked chicken	1 cup	250 mL
Finely chopped celery	3 tbsp.	50 mL
Onion powder	¼ tsp.	1 mL
Parsley flakes	½ tsp.	2 mL
Salt	¼ tsp.	1 mL
Light salad dressing (or mayonnaise)	3 tbsp.	50 mL
Milk	3 tbsp.	50 mL

Combine all 7 ingredients in small bowl. Mix well. Makes 1 cup (250 mL).

2 tbsp. (30 mL): 58 Calories; 2.3 g Total Fat; 146 mg Sodium; 8 g Protein; 1 g Carbohydrate; trace Dietary Fiber

CUCUMBER FILLING

Try this in Ribbon Sandwiches, page 29, or in Toast Cups, page 105.

Light cream cheese	4 oz.	125 g
Finely diced cucumber	1/3 cup	75 mL
Non-fat sour cream	2 tbsp.	30 mL
Chopped chives	1 tsp.	5 mL
Salt, sprinkle		
Pepper, sprinkle		

Mix all 6 ingredients in small bowl. Makes about 3/4 cup (175 mL).

2 tbsp. (30 mL): 43 Calories; 3.3 g Total Fat; 192 mg Sodium; 2 g Protein; 1 g Carbohydrate; trace Dietary Fiber

Pictured on page 18 and page 72.

CRUNCHY EGG FILLING

Try using a pastry blender to chop up the hard-boiled eggs. A great filling for Ribbon Sandwiches, page 29, or Toast Cups, page 105.

Large hard-boiled eggs, chopped	3	3
Finely chopped cucumber, with peel	1/2 cup	125 mL
Grated carrot	2 tbsp.	30 mL
Low-fat Thousand Island (or your favorite creamy) dressing	1 1/2 tbsp.	25 mL
Salt, sprinkle		
Pepper, sprinkle		

Combine all 6 ingredients in small bowl. Mix well. Makes 1 1/3 cups (325 mL).

2 tbsp. (30 mL): 27 Calories; 1.8 g Total Fat; 41 mg Sodium; 2 g Protein; 1 g Carbohydrate; trace Dietary Fiber

Pictured on page 18 and page 72.

HAM FILLING

The relish gives this filling a little bit of crunch.

Cans of ham flakes (6 1/2 oz.,184 g, each), drained	2	2
Sweet pickle relish	2 tbsp.	30 mL
Onion flakes, crushed	1 tsp.	5 mL
Light salad dressing (or mayonnaise)	3 tbsp.	50 mL

Mix all 4 ingredients in small bowl. Makes about 1 1/3 cups (325 mL).

2 tbsp. (30 mL): 95 Calories; 7.4 g Total Fat; 500 mg Sodium; 5 g Protein; 1 g Carbohydrate; trace Dietary Fiber

EGG FILLING

An old favorite.

Large hard-boiled eggs, chopped	6	6
Finely chopped celery	2 tbsp.	30 mL
Salt	1/2 tsp.	2 mL
Parsley flakes	1/2 tsp.	2 mL
Onion powder	1/4 tsp.	1 mL
Light salad dressing (or mayonnaise)	1/4 cup	60 mL

Mix all 6 ingredients in medium bowl. Makes about 1 3/4 cups (425 mL).

2 tbsp. (30 mL): 45 Calories; 3.3 g Total Fat; 153 mg Sodium; 3 g Protein; 1 g Carbohydrate; trace Dietary Fiber

Pictured on page 17.

FLAVORED CREAM CHEESE SPREAD

Serve with Bagels, page 19, Pumpernickel Bread, page 9, or any whole wheat or rye breads.

Light cream cheese, softened	4 oz.	125 g

FLAVORINGS

Garlic powder	¼ tsp.	1 mL
Grated Parmesan cheese	2 tbsp.	30 mL
Liquid honey	¼ cup	60 mL
Orange marmalade	¼ cup	60 mL
Maple-flavored syrup	1 tbsp.	15 mL
Frozen concentrated orange juice	1 tbsp.	15 mL

Beat cream cheese in small bowl until quite soft.

Flavorings: Add 1 flavoring. Mix well. Makes ½ cup (125 mL).

1 tbsp. (15 mL) with honey: 106 Calories; 3 g Total Fat; 173 mg Sodium; 2 g Protein; 19 g Carbohydrate; 1 g Dietary Fiber

CREAM BLUE SPREAD

Blue cheese flavor is quite mild. An excellent spread.

Light cream cheese, softened	4 oz.	125 g
Crumbled blue cheese	2 tbsp.	30 mL
Light salad dressing (or mayonnaise)	⅓ cup	75 mL
Finely chopped walnuts	½ cup	125 mL
Worcestershire sauce	½ tsp.	2 mL
Onion salt	⅛ tsp.	0.5 mL

Mix all 6 ingredients in small bowl. Makes about 1 cup (250 mL).

1 tbsp. (15 mL): 59 Calories; 5.3 g Total Fat; 136 mg Sodium; 2 g Protein; 2 g Carbohydrate; trace Dietary Fiber

CREAM PEPPER SPREAD

Why use plain cream cheese when you can spice it up?

Light cream cheese, softened	4 oz.	125 g
Margarine	¼ cup	60 mL
Chili sauce (or ketchup)	2 tbsp.	30 mL
Chopped green pepper	2 tbsp.	30 mL
Light salad dressing (or mayonnaise)	2 tbsp.	30 mL

Mix all 5 ingredients in small bowl. Makes about 1 cup (250 mL).

1 tbsp. (15 mL): 49 Calories; 4.6 g Total Fat; 152 mg Sodium; 1 g Protein; 1 g Carbohydrate; trace Dietary Fiber

Pictured on page 72.

CREAM ONION SPREAD

Good onion flavor.

Light cream cheese, softened	4 oz.	125 g
Chopped chives	2 tbsp.	30 mL
Milk	1 tsp.	5 mL
Salt, sprinkle		
Pepper, sprinkle		

Mash all 5 ingredients in small bowl. Makes about ½ cup (125 mL).

1 tbsp. (15 mL): 31 Calories; 2.5 g Total Fat; 143 mg Sodium; 2 g Protein; 1 g Carbohydrate; trace Dietary Fiber

CREAM OLIVE SPREAD

A good olive flavor.

Light cream cheese, softened	4 oz.	125 g
Chopped pimiento-stuffed olives	2 tbsp.	30 mL
Chopped celery	1 tsp.	5 mL
Chopped green pepper	1 tsp.	5 mL
Chopped green onion	1 tsp.	5 mL

Mix all 5 ingredients in small bowl. Makes about ½ cup (125 mL).

1 tbsp. (15 mL): 34 Calories; 2.8 g Total Fat; 192 mg Sodium; 2 g Protein; 1 g Carbohydrate; trace Dietary Fiber

OLIVE NUT FILLING

This is definitely for olive lovers.

Chopped walnuts	½ cup	125 mL
Shredded lettuce, lightly packed	½ cup	125 mL
Chopped pimiento-stuffed olives	½ cup	125 mL
Light salad dressing (or mayonnaise)	¼ cup	60 mL

Stir all 4 ingredients in small bowl. Makes about 1 cup (250 mL).

1 tbsp. (15 mL): 41 Calories; 3.9 g Total Fat; 127 mg Sodium; 1 g Protein; 1 g Carbohydrate; trace Dietary Fiber

Pictured on page 17.

CREAM FRUIT SPREAD

Delicious on raisin or nut bread.

Light cream cheese, softened	4 oz.	125 g
Milk	¼ cup	60 mL
Lemon juice	½ tsp.	2 mL
Chopped dates	⅓ cup	75 mL
Chopped dried apricots	¼ cup	60 mL
Chopped raisins	¼ cup	60 mL
Chopped pecans (or walnuts), optional	¼ cup	60 mL

Combine cream cheese, milk and lemon juice in medium bowl.

Add remaining 4 ingredients. Mix. Makes about 1⅓ cups (325 mL).

1 tbsp. (15 mL): 28 Calories; 1 g Total Fat; 56 mg Sodium; 1 g Protein; 4 g Carbohydrate; trace Dietary Fiber

Pictured on page 17.

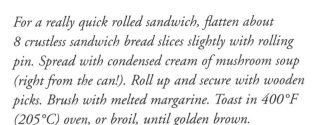

For a really quick rolled sandwich, flatten about 8 crustless sandwich bread slices slightly with rolling pin. Spread with condensed cream of mushroom soup (right from the can!). Roll up and secure with wooden picks. Brush with melted margarine. Toast in 400°F (205°C) oven, or broil, until golden brown.

TUNA FILLING

Just the way you like it.

Can of tuna, drained and flaked	6½ oz.	184 g
Finely chopped celery	¼ cup	60 mL
Onion flakes	1 tsp.	5 mL
Salt	⅛ tsp.	0.5 mL
Light salad dressing (or mayonnaise)	¼ cup	60 mL

Mix all 5 ingredients in small bowl. Makes 1 cup (250 mL).

1 tbsp. (15 mL): 25 Calories; 1.2 g Total Fat; 91 mg Sodium; 3 g Protein; 1 g Carbohydrate; trace Dietary Fiber

TUNA CHEESE FILLING

It's hard to beat taste combined with economy.

Can of tuna, drained and flaked	6½ oz.	184 g
Light cream cheese, softened	4 oz.	125 g
Margarine, softened	2 tsp.	10 mL
Finely chopped onion	½ cup	125 mL
Lemon juice	1 tsp.	5 mL
Salt	⅛ tsp.	0.5 mL
Pepper	⅛ tsp.	0.5 mL
Ground walnuts (optional)	½ cup	125 mL

Mash all 8 ingredients in small bowl. Makes a scant 2 cups (500 mL).

1 tbsp. (15 mL): 17 Calories; 1 g Total Fat; 67 mg Sodium; 2 g Protein; trace Carbohydrate; trace Dietary Fiber

SALMON FILLING

Can't go wrong with this sandwich.

Can of red salmon, drained, skin and round bones removed	7½ oz.	213 g
Onion flakes	½ tsp.	2 mL
Parsley flakes	½ tsp.	2 mL
Salt	¼ tsp.	1 mL
Light salad dressing (or mayonnaise)	¼ cup	60 mL

Mix all 5 ingredients in small bowl. Makes 1 cup (250 mL).

1 tbsp. (15 mL): 29 Calories; 1.6 g Total Fat; 130 mg Sodium; 3 g Protein; 1 g Carbohydrate; trace Dietary Fiber

SALMON CHEDDAR SPREAD

An old standby for cheese lovers.

Can of red salmon, drained, skin and round bones removed	7½ oz.	213 g
Grated light Cheddar cheese	½ cup	125 mL
Chopped celery	¼ cup	60 mL
Onion flakes, crushed	2 tsp.	10 mL
Light salad dressing (or mayonnaise)	2 tbsp.	30 mL

Mix all 5 ingredients in small bowl. Makes about 1 cup (250 mL).

1 tbsp. (15 mL): 34 Calories; 1.8 g Total Fat; 97 mg Sodium; 4 g Protein; 1 g Carbohydrate; trace Dietary Fiber

SMOKED SALMON FILLING

An expensive flavor for an ordinary price. Spread on croissants, crackers, dark rye or pumpernickel bread.

Light cream cheese, softened	**4 oz.**	**125 g**
Finely chopped onion	**1 tbsp.**	**15 mL**
Lemon juice	**1 tsp.**	**5 mL**
Prepared horseradish	**½ tsp.**	**2 mL**
Salt	**⅛ tsp.**	**0.5 mL**
Liquid smoke	**½ tsp.**	**2 mL**
Can of red salmon, drained, skin and round bones removed	**7½ oz.**	**213 g**

Mix first 6 ingredients in small bowl.

Mix in salmon. Makes about 1½ cups (375 mL).

1 tbsp. (15 mL): 22 Calories; 1.3 g Total Fat; 101 mg Sodium; 2 g Protein; trace Carbohydrate; trace Dietary Fiber

Pictured on page 18.

BEAN FILLING

So much protein. So little cost.

Can of navy (or pinto) beans, drained	**14 oz.**	**398 mL**
Sweet pickle relish	**2 tbsp.**	**30 mL**
Salad dressing (or mayonnaise)	**2 tbsp.**	**30 mL**
Chili sauce (or ketchup)	**1 tbsp.**	**15 mL**

Combine all 4 ingredients in small bowl. Mash. Bottom of drinking glass works well. Makes about 1⅓ cups (325 mL).

⅓ cup (75 mL): 142 Calories; 4.1 g Total Fat; 81 mg Sodium; 6 g Protein; 21 g Carbohydrate; 3 g Dietary Fiber

SHRIMP CREAM SPREAD

It's so easy to keep ingredients on hand for this filling.

Can of shrimp, drained and rinsed	**4 oz.**	**113 g**
Light cream cheese, softened	**4 oz.**	**125 g**
Chili sauce	**1 tsp.**	**5 mL**
Lemon juice	**½ tsp.**	**2 mL**
Worcestershire sauce	**½ tsp.**	**2 mL**
Garlic powder	**1/16 tsp.**	**0.5 mL**
Light salad dressing (or mayonnaise)	**2 tbsp.**	**30 mL**
Dill weed	**⅛ tsp.**	**0.5 mL**

Mash all 8 ingredients in small bowl. Makes about 1 cup (250 mL).

1 tbsp. (15 mL): 28 Calories; 1.8 g Total Fat; 102 mg Sodium; 2 g Protein; 1 g Carbohydrate; trace Dietary Fiber

Pictured on page 17.

TANGY BEEF SPREAD

Horseradish flavor is very mild.

Ground cooked roast beef	**2 cups**	**500 mL**
Light salad dressing (or mayonnaise)	**¼ cup**	**60 mL**
Prepared horseradish	**1 tsp.**	**5 mL**
Milk (or water)	**¼ cup**	**60 mL**
Salt	**¼ tsp.**	**1 mL**

Mix all 5 ingredients in small bowl. Makes about 2 cups (500 mL).

2 tbsp. (30 mL): 51 Calories; 2.2 g Total Fat; 87 mg Sodium; 7 g Protein; 1 g Carbohydrate; trace Dietary Fiber

Pictured on page 17.

Sandwiches

Classic, trendy, artistic, colorful and hearty, are just a few ways to describe the venerable sandwich. Although a sandwich, by definition, is simply two pieces of bread with something in the middle, the combinations of breads and fillings are endless. Take a look at the collection of recipes in this section and make a point of trying a different sandwich every time.

CHICKEN ASPARAGUS SANDWICH

Wonderfully fresh tasting.

Margarine	2 tsp.	10 mL
White (or whole wheat) bread slices	2	2
Process light Cheddar cheese slice	1	1
Cooked sliced chicken	2 oz.	57 g
Salt, sprinkle		
Pepper, sprinkle		
Fresh asparagus spears, cooked	4	4

Spread margarine on both bread slices.

Layer cheese slice, chicken slices, salt and pepper on 1 bread slice. Lay asparagus spears over chicken. Place second bread slice over asparagus. Makes 1.

1 sandwich: 390 Calories; 15.8 g Total Fat; 564 mg Sodium; 29 g Protein; 31 g Carbohydrate; 2 g Dietary Fiber

Pictured on page 72.

CHICKEN HAM SANDWICH

A great way to use up Sunday leftovers.

Margarine	2 tsp.	10 mL
White (or whole wheat) bread slices	2	2
Cooked chicken slice	1	1
Salt, sprinkle		
Pepper, sprinkle		
Ham slice	1	1
Lettuce leaf	1	1
Cranberry sauce	1 tbsp.	15 mL

Spread margarine on both bread slices. Layer chicken slice, salt, pepper, ham and lettuce on 1 slice. Spread cranberry sauce on second slice. Place over lettuce. Makes 1.

1 sandwich: 36 Calories; 12.3 g Total Fat; 922 mg Sodium; 21 g Protein; 36 g Carbohydrate; 1 g Dietary Fiber

CHICKEN SANDWICH

A good full sandwich. For fewer calories, half the amount of chicken may be used.

Margarine	1½ tsp.	7 mL
Whole wheat (or white) bread slices	2	2
Cooked boneless, skinless chicken breast, sliced	2 oz.	57 g
Pepper, sprinkle		
Lettuce leaves	2	2
Light salad dressing (or mayonnaise)	1½ tsp.	7 mL

Spread margarine on both bread slices. Layer chicken, pepper and lettuce on 1 slice.

Spread salad dressing on second bread slice. Place second slice over lettuce. Cut in half diagonally. Makes 1.

1 sandwich: 308 Calories; 8 g Total Fat; 470 mg Sodium; 23 g Protein; 30 g Carbohydrate; 3 g Dietary Fiber

CORNED BEEF SANDWICH

Right out of the deli.

Margarine	2 tsp.	10 mL
Rye bread slices (light or dark)	2	2
Shaved deli corned beef	2 oz.	57 g
Lettuce leaf	1	1
Prepared mustard	½ tsp.	2 mL
Prepared horseradish	¼ tsp.	1 mL

Spread margarine on both bread slices. Pile corned beef on 1 bread slice. Cover with lettuce leaf.

Mix mustard and horseradish in small bowl. Spread on second bread slice. Place over lettuce. Makes 1.

1 sandwich: 371 Calories; 19.2 g Total Fat; 1142 mg Sodium; 16 g Protein; 35 g Carbohydrate; 4 g Dietary Fiber

VEGETARIAN SANDWICH

Full, thick and appetizing.

Margarine	1½ tsp.	7 mL
Whole wheat (or white) bread slices	2	2
Medium tomato slices	2	2
Thinly sliced cucumber	¼ cup	60 mL
Pepper, sprinkle		
Grated carrot	2 tbsp.	30 mL
Alfalfa sprouts (optional)	¼ cup	60 mL
Lettuce leaves	2	2
Light salad dressing (or mayonnaise)	1 tsp.	5 mL

Spread margarine on both bread slices.

Layer tomato, cucumber, pepper, carrot, alfalfa sprouts and lettuce on 1 slice.

Spread salad dressing on second bread slice. Place second slice over first. Cut in half diagonally. Makes 1.

1 sandwich: 222 Calories; 8.6 g Total Fat; 413 mg Sodium; 6 g Protein; 33 g Carbohydrate; 4 g Dietary Fiber

If lettuce, parsley, celery or even carrots are wilted and blemished, remove any brown edges or spots, sprinkle with cold water, wrap in a tea towel and chill for 1 hour or so.

HAM SWISS SNACK

For rye bread lovers.

Margarine	2 tsp.	10 mL
Rye bread slices (light or dark)	2	2
Cooked ham slices	2	2
Swiss cheese slice	1	1
Medium tomato slices	2	2
Lettuce leaf	1	1
Prepared mustard	1 tsp.	5 mL
Light salad dressing (or mayonnaise), optional		

Spread margarine on both bread slices. Layer ham, Swiss cheese, tomato and lettuce on 1 bread slice.

Spread mustard and salad dressing over second slice. Place over lettuce. Makes 1.

1 sandwich: 429 Calories; 19.8 g Total Fat; 1666 mg Sodium; 26 g Protein; 38 g Carbohydrate; 4 g Dietary Fiber

HAM SANDWICH

For white bread lovers.

Margarine	2 tsp.	10 mL
White (or whole wheat) bread slices	2	2
Cooked ham slices	2	2
Process light Cheddar cheese slice	1	1
Lettuce leaf	1	1
Light salad dressing (or mayonnaise)	2 tsp.	10 mL
Prepared mustard	1 tsp.	5 mL

Spread margarine on both bread slices. Layer ham, cheese and lettuce on 1 slice.

Spread salad dressing and mustard on other slice. Place over lettuce. Makes 1.

1 sandwich: 411 Calories; 20 g Total Fat; 1687 mg Sodium; 24 g Protein; 32 g Carbohydrate; 1 g Dietary Fiber

HAM AND CUKE SANDWICH

Yummy to eat for lunch any day of the week.

Light salad dressing (or mayonnaise)	2 tsp.	10 mL
Low-fat French (or Russian) dressing	2 tsp.	10 mL
White (or whole wheat) bread slices	2	2
Shaved ham slices (about 2 oz., 57 g)	3	3
Cucumber slices, with peel	3-4	3-4

Combine salad dressing and French dressing in small bowl. Mix well.

Spread mixture on both bread slices.

Place ham slices on 1 slice of bread. Top with cucumber slices. Place second bread slice over cucumber. Cut in half. Makes 1.

1 sandwich: 276 Calories; 8.3 g Total Fat; 1375 mg Sodium; 16 g Protein; 33 g Carbohydrate; 1 g Dietary Fiber

Pictured on page 71.

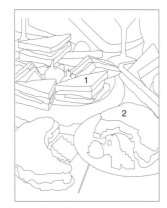

1. Ham And Cuke Sandwich, this page
2. Crab Salad Sandwiches, page 78

TOMATO CHEESE SANDWICH

A red and white lunch. Very good.

Margarine	1½ tsp.	7 mL
Whole wheat bread slices	2	2
Process skim mozzarella cheese slice	1	1
Medium tomato slices	2	2
Alfalfa sprouts (optional)	¼ cup	60 mL
Lettuce leaves	2	2
Light salad dressing (or mayonnaise)	1½ tsp.	7 mL

Spread margarine on bread slices.

Layer next 4 ingredients in order given on 1 slice.

Spread other slice with salad dressing. Place over lettuce. Cut sandwich in half diagonally. Makes 1.

1 sandwich: *286 Calories; 11.6 g Total Fat; 435 mg Sodium; 13 g Protein; 32 g Carbohydrate; 4 g Dietary Fiber*

Pictured on page 72.

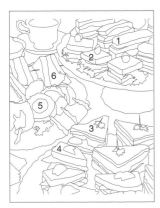

Props Courtesy Of: Stokes

CUCUMBER SANDWICH

Available year-round, cucumbers make a light addition to any sandwich.

Margarine	2 tsp.	10 mL
White (or whole wheat) bread slices	2	2
Thin cucumber slices	4-6	4-6
Salt, sprinkle		
Pepper, sprinkle		
Alfalfa sprouts	¼ cup	60 mL
Light salad dressing (or mayonnaise), optional		

Spread margarine on both bread slices. Cover 1 slice with cucumber slices. Sprinkle with salt and pepper. Lay alfalfa sprouts over top. Spread second slice of bread with salad dressing. Place over sprouts. Cut and serve. Makes 1.

1 sandwich: *226 Calories; 9.5 g Total Fat; 387 mg Sodium; 5 g Protein; 30 g Carbohydrate; 2 g Dietary Fiber*

Pictured on page 72.

ONION RETREAT

Eating one of these onion sandwiches makes being alone worthwhile.

Margarine	2 tsp.	10 mL
Bread slices	2	2
Large Spanish onion slice	1	1
Salt, sprinkle		
Pepper, sprinkle		

Spread margarine on both bread slices. Cover 1 slice with onion. Sprinkle with salt and pepper. Makes 1.

1 sandwich: *222 Calories; 9.4 g Total Fat; 386 mg Sodium; 5 g Protein; 29 g Carbohydrate; 1 g Dietary Fiber*

PEANUT BACON SNACK

An unusual combination that you're sure to like!

White (or whole wheat) bread slices	2	2
Smooth peanut butter	1 tbsp.	15 mL
Bacon slice, cooked crisp and crumbled	1	1
Marmalade (or jelly)	1 tbsp.	15 mL

Spread 1 slice with peanut butter. Sprinkle bacon over top. Spread marmalade on second slice. Place over bacon. Makes 1.

1 sandwich: 334 Calories; 13 g Total Fat; 465 mg Sodium; 11 g Protein; 46 g Carbohydrate; 3 g Dietary Fiber

PEANUT BUTTER SANDWICHES

Most everyone loves this combination.

Margarine	2¹/₂ tbsp.	37 mL
White (or whole wheat) bread slices	8	8
Smooth peanut butter	2 tbsp.	30 mL
Medium bananas, sliced	2	2

Spread margarine on bread slices. Cover 4 slices with peanut butter. Arrange banana slices over top. Place remaining 4 slices over banana. Cut in half. Makes 4.

1 sandwich: 314 Calories; 13.2 g Total Fat; 418 mg Sodium; 8 g Protein; 43 g Carbohydrate; 2 g Dietary Fiber

Variation: Jelly, jam or honey may be added.

PEANUT CRANBERRY SNACK

For something entirely different.

Margarine	2 tsp.	10 mL
Raisin bread slices	2	2
Cranberry sauce	1 tbsp.	15 mL
Peanut butter (smooth or crunchy)	1 tbsp.	15 mL
Lettuce leaf	1	1

Spread margarine on bread slices. Spread 1 slice with cranberry sauce and the other with peanut butter. Place lettuce over cranberry sauce. Place other slice over top. Makes 1.

1 sandwich: 323 Calories; 17.2 g Total Fat; 369 mg Sodium; 8 g Protein; 37 g Carbohydrate; 3 g Dietary Fiber

Before taking dishes to picnics, clubs, etc., mark them with fingernail polish. It won't come off when washed, but can be removed with fingernail polish remover.

PEANUT BUTTER AND PICKLE SANDWICH

Who would have thought! Interesting and very tasty!

Peanut butter (smooth or crunchy)	2 tbsp.	30 mL
White (or whole wheat) bread slices	2	2
Dill pickles, cut in half lengthwise	2	2

Spread peanut butter on each bread slice.

Lay pickle halves on paper towel for 1 to 2 minutes to soak up juice. Lay pickle halves on top of peanut butter. Place second slice of bread over pickle. Cut in half. Makes 1.

1 sandwich: 359 Calories; 18.2 g Total Fat; 1689 mg Sodium; 13 g Protein; 39 g Carbohydrate; 4 g Dietary Fiber

Variation: Spread peanut butter on flour tortilla. Lay small whole dill pickle on top of tortilla at one end. Roll tortilla around pickle.

THE "NEW" PEANUT BUTTER SANDWICH

Alfalfa sprouts give peanut butter sandwiches a new kick! Great to wash down with a big glass of milk.

Peanut butter (smooth or crunchy)	2 tbsp.	30 mL
White (or whole wheat) bagel, cut in half	1	1
Jam (your favorite)	2 tsp.	10 mL
Liquid honey	1 tsp.	5 mL
Packed alfalfa sprouts (optional)	½ cup	125 mL

Spread peanut butter on each bagel half. Spread 1 bagel half with jam and honey. Top with alfalfa sprouts. Place second bagel half over sprouts. Press down. Cut in half. Makes 1.

1 sandwich: 501 Calories; 17.8 g Total Fat; 871 mg Sodium; 17 g Protein; 72 g Carbohydrate; 2 g Dietary Fiber

---

To make a bag lunch more fun for smaller children include:

- *a cartoon that they can understand and appreciate the humor*
- *a simple note or message drawing (rebus)*
- *a cookie, or other treat they don't normally get*

DILL PICKLE SANDWICH

If you like dill pickles, you will love this sandwich!

Light salad dressing (or mayonnaise)	1 tbsp.	15 mL
White (or whole wheat) bread slices	2	2
Medium-size dill pickles, sliced lengthwise	2	2

Spread salad dressing on 1 side of each bread slice.

Lay dill pickle slices on 1 bread slice. Top with other slice of bread. Cut in half on cutting board. Makes 1.

1 sandwich: 211 Calories; 5.8 g Total Fat; 1649 mg Sodium; 5 g Protein; 35 g Carbohydrate; 2 g Dietary Fiber

Pictured on front cover.

Variation: Spread bread slices with prepared mustard instead of light salad dressing or mayonnaise.

QUICK BANANA SANDWICH

A new "look" to the traditional peanut butter and banana sandwich.

Peanut butter (smooth or crunchy)	1 tbsp.	15 mL
Jam (your favorite)	2 tsp.	10 mL
White (or whole wheat) bread slice	1	1
Ripe small banana	1	1

Spread peanut butter and jam on bread slice. Lay banana diagonally across middle of slice. Bring opposite corners up and fasten with wooden pick. Makes 1.

1 sandwich: 277 Calories; 9.4 g Total Fat; 222 mg Sodium; 7 g Protein; 45 g Carbohydrate; 3 g Dietary Fiber

Variation: For a quick cocktail sandwich, fold as above then cut into $\frac{1}{2}$ inch (12 mm) slices and secure individually with cocktail picks.

Pictured on page 72.

CREAM CHEESE AND GRAPE JELLY SANDWICH

This is very quick and easy to make for lunch.

Light spreadable cream cheese	2 tbsp.	30 mL
White (or whole wheat) bread slices	2	2
Grape jelly	4 tsp.	20 mL

Spread cream cheese on each slice of bread. Spread jelly on top of cream cheese on 1 slice. Top with second slice of bread. Cut in half on cutting board. Makes 1.

1 sandwich: 286 Calories; 6.8 g Total Fat; 573 mg Sodium; 8 g Protein; 48 g Carbohydrate; 1 g Dietary Fiber

Pictured on front cover.

SCRAMBLED EGG SANDWICHES

A wonderful last minute sandwich. A family favorite. Try it with cheese and ketchup. Not recommended for freezing.

Margarine	2$\frac{1}{2}$ tbsp.	37 mL
White (or whole wheat) bread slices	8	8
Process cheese spread	1 tbsp.	15 mL
Ketchup	1 tbsp.	15 mL
Margarine	1 tbsp.	15 mL
Large eggs	6	6
Water	3 tbsp.	50 mL
Salt, sprinkle		
Pepper, sprinkle		

Spread first amount of margarine on bread slices. Spread 2 slices with cheese spread and 2 with ketchup.

Heat second amount of margarine in frying pan. Add eggs and water. Break yolks and stir until eggs are cooked but not dry. Sprinkle with salt and pepper. Spoon onto 4 plain buttered bread slices. Cover with cheese and ketchup bread slices. Cut in half. Place 1 cheese and 1 ketchup portion on each plate or 2 of the same if desired. Makes 4.

1 sandwich: 368 Calories; 20.2 g Total Fat; 624 mg Sodium; 15 g Protein; 31 g Carbohydrate; 1 g Dietary Fiber

TUNA SALAD SANDWICHES

A crispy, crunchy sandwich with lots of flavor. Do not freeze.

Can of tuna, drained and flaked	6$\frac{1}{2}$ oz.	184 g
Large hard-boiled egg, chopped	1	1
Finely chopped celery	$\frac{1}{2}$ cup	125 mL
Light salad dressing (or mayonnaise)	6 tbsp.	100 mL
Salt	$\frac{1}{8}$ tsp.	0.5 mL
Paprika	$\frac{1}{4}$ tsp.	1 mL
Onion powder	$\frac{1}{8}$ tsp.	0.5 mL
Margarine	2$\frac{1}{2}$ tbsp.	37 mL
White (or whole wheat) bread slices	8	8

Mix tuna, egg and celery in medium bowl.

Stir next 4 ingredients in small bowl. Add to tuna mixture. Stir. Makes 1$\frac{1}{4}$ cups (300 mL) filling.

Spread margarine on bread slices. Divide and spread tuna mixture on 4 slices. Place remaining 4 slices over filling. Makes 4.

1 sandwich: 353 Calories; 16.9 g Total Fat; 819 mg Sodium; 17 g Protein; 33 g Carbohydrate; 1 g Dietary Fiber

To cut hard-boiled eggs into smooth slices, dip the knife into hot water between cuts.

SALMON SANDWICHES

Contains no salad dressing.

Can of red salmon, drained, skin and round bones removed	7½ oz.	213 g
Light cream cheese, softened	4 oz.	125 g
Grated cucumber, well drained	⅓ cup	75 mL
Finely chopped celery	3 tbsp.	50 mL
Dried chives	1 tsp.	5 mL
Onion powder	¼ tsp.	1 mL
Salt	¼ tsp.	1 mL
Margarine	¼ cup	60 mL
White (or whole wheat) bread slices	12	12

Mash salmon and cream cheese together in small bowl.

Add next 5 ingredients. Stir. Chill for at least 1 hour to firm cream cheese. Makes about 2 cups (500 mL) filling.

Spread margarine on bread slices. Divide and spread filling on 6 slices. Place remaining 6 slices over filling. Cut into 3 or 4 pieces each. Makes 6.

1 sandwich: 177 Calories; 8.5 g Total Fat; 490 mg Sodium; 8 g Protein; 17 g Carbohydrate; 1 g Dietary Fiber

CRAB SALAD SANDWICHES

Looks and tastes yummy. Adding lettuce to the filling makes it crunchy.

Frozen crabmeat, thawed (or 1 can, 4¼ oz., 120 g, drained), cartilage removed	1 cup	250 mL
Light salad dressing (or mayonnaise)	⅓ cup	75 mL
Onion powder	⅛ tsp.	0.5 mL
Paprika	¼ tsp.	1 mL
Dill weed	⅛ tsp.	0.5 mL
Lemon juice	1 tsp.	5 mL
Parsley flakes	½ tsp.	2 mL
Shredded lettuce, lightly packed	2 cups	500 mL
Margarine	2½ tbsp.	37 mL
Whole wheat (or pumpernickel or rye) bread slices	8	8

Mix first 8 ingredients in medium bowl. Makes about 2 cups (500 mL) filling.

Spread margarine on bread slices. Divide and spread filling on 4 slices. Place second slice over filling. Cut into 2 or 3 pieces each. Makes 4.

1 sandwich: 282 Calories; 14.1 g Total Fat; 747 mg Sodium; 10 g Protein; 32 g Carbohydrate; 4 g Dietary Fiber

Pictured on page 71.

Stratas

tratas are a wonderful hot dish that can be made in advance and kept in the refrigerator overnight. Bake your strata the next day and you have an exceptional variation on the traditional sandwich. It's a perfect meal to serve for brunch or lunch.

CHICKEN STRATA

Ready-made comfort food.

Ground chicken	1½ lbs.	680 g
Finely chopped onion	½ cup	125 mL
Diced green pepper	¼ cup	60 mL
Cooking oil	2 tsp.	10 mL
Salt, sprinkle		
Pepper, sprinkle		
White (or whole wheat) bread slices, crusts removed	12	12
Frozen peas, thawed	2 cups	500 mL
Process light Cheddar cheese slices	6	6
Large eggs	5	5
Condensed cream of mushroom soup	10 oz.	284 mL
Milk	1¾ cups	425 mL
Poultry seasoning	¼ tsp.	1 mL

Scramble-fry ground chicken, onion and green pepper in cooking oil in frying pan until chicken is no longer pink. Drain. Sprinkle with salt and pepper.

Cover bottom of greased 9 × 13 inch (22 × 33 cm) pan with 6 bread slices. Layer with chicken mixture, peas, cheese slices and remaining 6 bread slices.

Beat eggs in medium bowl until smooth. Add remaining 3 ingredients. Mix. Pour over top of bread. Cover. Chill for 3 hours or overnight. Bake, uncovered, in 350°F (175°C) oven for about 1 hour until set. Serves 8.

1 serving: 371 Calories; 10.4 g Total Fat; 871 mg Sodium; 35 g Protein; 33 g Carbohydrate; 2 g Dietary Fiber

TURKEY STRATA

This will remind you of a hot turkey salad sandwich.

White (or whole wheat) bread slices, with crusts	12	12
Grated medium Cheddar cheese	1 cup	250 mL
Light salad dressing (or mayonnaise)	½ cup	125 mL
Sweet pickle relish	¼ cup	60 mL
Finely chopped cooked turkey	2 cups	500 mL
Large eggs	6	6
Salt	¾ tsp.	4 mL
Pepper	⅛ tsp.	0.5 mL
Milk	2¾ cups	675 mL
Toasted sliced almonds (optional), see Tip, page 61	⅓ cup	75 mL

Cover bottom of greased 9 × 13 inch (22 × 33 cm) pan with 6 bread slices.

Stir next 4 ingredients together in medium bowl. Spread over bread layer. Cover with remaining 6 bread slices.

Beat eggs, salt and pepper in medium bowl. Stir in milk. Pour over top. Cover. Chill for several hours or overnight. Cover. Bake in 350°F (175°C) oven for 45 to 50 minutes.

Sprinkle with almonds. Bake, uncovered, for about 15 minutes. Serves 8.

1 serving: 404 Calories; 18.5 g Total Fat; 824 mg Sodium; 28 g Protein; 32 g Carbohydrate; 2 g Dietary Fiber

BAKED SANDWICHES

Ham, cheese and eggs. A great winter day "sandwich."

Can of ham flakes, drained	6½ oz.	184 g
Grated Swiss cheese	2 cups	500 mL
Light salad dressing (or mayonnaise)	⅓ cup	75 mL
Prepared mustard	1 tsp.	5 mL
Onion flakes	1 tbsp.	15 mL
Parsley flakes	1 tsp.	5 mL
White (or whole wheat) bread slices, with crusts	12	12
Large eggs	6	6
Milk	2½ cups	625 mL
Salt	½ tsp.	2 mL
Pepper	⅛ tsp.	0.5 mL

Mix first 6 ingredients in medium bowl.

Cover bottom of greased 9 × 13 inch (22 × 33 cm) pan with 6 bread slices. Spread ham mixture over top. Cover with remaining 6 bread slices.

Beat eggs in large bowl until frothy. Mix in milk, salt and pepper. Pour over top of bread. Cover. Chill overnight. Bake, uncovered, in 350°F (175°C) oven for 30 to 40 minutes until set. Serves 8.

1 serving: 398 Calories; 20.8 g Total Fat; 947 mg Sodium; 23 g Protein; 29 g Carbohydrate; 1 g Dietary Fiber

SAUSAGE STRATA

Very attractive. Mustard gives an added zip.

White (or whole wheat) bread slices, with crusts	8	8
Sausage meat	1 lb.	454 g
Chopped onion	1 cup	250 mL
Diced green pepper	1 cup	250 mL
Grated sharp Cheddar cheese	1 cup	250 mL
Large eggs	4	4
Can of skim evaporated milk	13½ oz.	385 mL
Prepared mustard	1 tbsp.	15 mL
Seasoned salt	½ tsp.	2 mL
Pepper	1/16 tsp.	0.5 mL
Crushed cornflakes cereal	½ cup	125 mL
Margarine, melted	1 tbsp.	15 mL

Cover bottom of greased 9 × 9 inch (22 × 22 cm) pan with 4 bread slices.

Scramble-fry sausage meat in frying pan for 3 minutes. Add onion and green pepper. Scramble-fry for 2 minutes until sausage is no longer pink and onion is soft. Drain. Sprinkle over bread layer.

Sprinkle with cheese. Cover with remaining 4 bread slices.

Beat eggs in small bowl. Add next 4 ingredients. Mix well. Pour over top of bread. Pan will be very full.

Stir cornflake crumbs into margarine in small bowl. Sprinkle over top. Bake, uncovered, in 350°F (175°C) oven for 40 minutes until set. Serves 6.

1 serving: 503 Calories; 26.3 g Total Fat; 993 mg Sodium; 24 g Protein; 42 g Carbohydrate; 2 g Dietary Fiber

ZIPPY STRATA

This will remind you of pizza. Red tomatoes add nice color.

White (or whole wheat) bread slices, with crusts	12	12
Part-skim mozzarella cheese slices	6	6
Medium tomato slices	15	15
Can of mushroom pieces, drained	10 oz.	284 mL
Onion flakes	3 tbsp.	50 mL
Large eggs	5	5
Salt	½ tsp.	2 mL
Pepper	1/8 tsp.	0.5 mL
Dried whole oregano	¾ tsp.	4 mL
Dried sweet basil	½ tsp.	2 mL
Garlic powder	¼ tsp.	1 mL
Cayenne pepper	¼ tsp.	1 mL
All-purpose flour	¼ cup	60 mL
Milk	3 cups	750 mL
Grated Parmesan cheese	½ cup	125 mL

Cover bottom of greased 9 × 13 inch (22 × 33 cm) pan with 6 slices. Layer with cheese slices, tomato, mushrooms, onion flakes and remaining 6 bread slices.

Beat eggs in medium bowl. Beat in next 8 ingredients. Pour over top.

Sprinkle with Parmesan cheese. Cover. Chill overnight. Bake, uncovered, in 325°F (160°C) oven for about 1¼ hours until set. Serves 8.

1 serving: 338 Calories; 13.5 g Total Fat; 768 mg Sodium; 20 g Protein; 34 g Carbohydrate; 2 g Dietary Fiber

HAM STRATAWICH

Very showy. Handy make-ahead for breakfast, brunch or lunch. Cut into "sandwiches."

Sliced onion	1 cup	250 mL
Cooking oil	1 tsp.	5 mL
White (or whole wheat) bread slices, with crusts	12	12
Frozen chopped broccoli, thawed, smaller pieces chopped	2½ cups	625 mL
Diced cooked ham	2 cups	500 mL
Grated medium Cheddar cheese	2 cups	500 mL
Large eggs	5	5
Milk	2½ cups	625 mL
Dry mustard	½ tsp.	2 mL
Salt	½ tsp.	2 mL
Pepper	¼ tsp.	1 mL
Garlic powder	¼ tsp.	1 mL
Onion powder	¼ tsp.	1 mL
Crushed cornflakes cereal	½ cup	125 mL
Margarine, melted	2 tbsp.	30 mL

Sauté onion in cooking oil in medium frying pan until soft.

Cover bottom of greased 9 × 13 inch (22 × 33 cm) pan with 6 bread slices. Layer with onion, broccoli, ham, cheese and remaining 6 bread slices.

Beat eggs in medium bowl until smooth. Add next 6 ingredients. Mix. Pour over top of bread.

Stir cornflake crumbs into margarine in small bowl. Sprinkle over egg mixture. Cover. Chill overnight. Bake, uncovered, in 325°F (160°C) oven for about 1 hour until set. Serves 8.

1 serving: 459 Calories; 23 g Total Fat; 1250 mg Sodium; 26 g Protein; 37 g Carbohydrate; 3 g Dietary Fiber

SAUSAGE STRATA

A hearty lunch.

White (or whole wheat) bread slices, with crusts	12	12
Grated light Cheddar cheese	2 cups	500 mL
Sausage meat	2 lbs.	900 g
Large eggs	8	8
Milk	2⅔ cups	650 mL
Salt	1 tsp.	5 mL
Pepper	¼ tsp.	1 mL
Onion powder	½ tsp.	2 mL
Worcestershire sauce	1 tsp.	5 mL
Dry mustard	½ tsp.	2 mL

Line bottom of greased 9 × 13 inch (22 × 33 cm) pan with 6 bread slices. Sprinkle with cheese.

Scramble-fry sausage meat in frying pan. Drain well. Sprinkle over cheese. Cover sausage with remaining 6 bread slices.

Beat eggs in large bowl. Add remaining 6 ingredients. Mix. Pour over top of bread. Cover. Chill overnight. Bake, uncovered, in 350°F (175°C) oven for about 1 hour until set. Serves 8.

1 serving: 503 Calories; 26.3 g Total Fat; 993 mg Sodium; 24 g Protein; 42 g Carbohydrate; 2 g Dietary Fiber

MUSHROOM STRATA

Actually a vegetable strata. Colorful.

Margarine	¼ cup	60 mL
Small fresh mushrooms, sliced	1 lb.	454 g
Diced celery	½ cup	125 mL
Diced green pepper	⅓ cup	75 mL
Finely chopped green onion	½ cup	125 mL
Grated carrot	½ cup	125 mL
Salad dressing (or mayonnaise)	½ cup	125 mL
Salt	¼ tsp.	1 mL
White (or whole wheat) bread slices, with crusts	8	8
Large eggs	3	3
Milk	2 cups	500 mL
Grated medium Cheddar cheese (optional)	½ cup	125 mL

Melt margarine in frying pan. Add next 5 ingredients. Sauté for 5 to 6 minutes until soft. This may need to be done in 2 batches. Remove from heat.

Stir in salad dressing and salt.

Cover bottom of greased 9 × 9 inch (22 × 22 cm) pan with 4 bread slices. Spread vegetable mixture over top. Cover with remaining 4 bread slices.

Beat eggs in medium bowl until frothy. Add milk. Beat well. Pour over bread. Cover. Chill overnight. Bake, uncovered, in 325°F (160°C) oven for 45 minutes.

Sprinkle with cheese. Bake for 15 minutes. Serves 6.

1 serving: 378 Calories; 23.3 g Total Fat; 607 mg Sodium; 11 g Protein; 32 g Carbohydrate; 2 g Dietary Fiber

To store fresh mushrooms, keep chilled, unwashed, in a paper bag or ventilated package for up to 5 days. If damp, wrap mushrooms in paper towels before storing. Use as soon as possible for best flavor.

Stuffed Sandwiches

stuffed sandwich can best be described as one where the filling is completely surrounded by the bread. Stuffed pitas, crescent rolls baked with filling inside, calzones, falafels, etc., are just a few examples of the impressive creations you can make with the recipes in this section.

BARBECUE BEEF BUNS

Great warm or cold. These freeze well. Simply take from the freezer and put it in your lunch bag. At lunchtime, warm in the microwave on high (100%) for one minute.

Lean ground beef	½ **lb.**	**225 g**
Small onion, cut into rings	**1**	**1**
Seasoned salt	½ **tsp.**	**2 mL**
Paprika	½ **tsp.**	**2 mL**
Regular (or smoky-flavored) barbecue sauce	½ **cup**	**125 mL**
Refrigerator crescent-style rolls (8 per tube)	8½ **oz.**	**235 g**

Scramble-fry ground beef in frying pan until almost brown. Add onion rings. Scramble-fry for 2 minutes until beef is no longer pink and onion is soft.

Stir in salt and paprika. Add barbecue sauce. Simmer, uncovered, for 10 minutes until liquid is evaporated. Cool.

Separate dough into 8 triangles. Spoon 2 tbsp. (30 mL) beef mixture onto each triangle. Bring the 3 points of each triangle to center over filling. Pinch all of edges together well to seal. Form into round shapes. Place each ball, seam side down, on ungreased baking sheet. Bake in 375°F (190°C) oven for 12 to 15 minutes until golden. Makes 8.

1 bun: 125 Calories; 7 g Total Fat; 380 mg Sodium; 7 g Protein; 8 g Carbohydrate; 1 g Dietary Fiber

PIZZA POP-UPS

Perfect for after basketball practice or for video movie night.

Tomato sauce	$\frac{1}{2}$ cup	125 mL
Chopped pepperoni	1 cup	250 mL
Finely chopped onion	1 tbsp.	15 mL
Grated Parmesan cheese	1 tbsp.	15 mL
Grated part-skim mozzarella cheese	$\frac{1}{2}$ cup	125 mL
Refrigerator flaky rolls (10 per tube)	12 oz.	340 g

Combine first 5 ingredients in small bowl. Mix.

Separate rolls into 20 pieces. Place 1 piece of dough into bottom of each of 10 greased muffin cups. Push down with finger to form shell (if dough sticks to your finger, coat finger with flour). Spoon pepperoni mixture into shells. Flatten remaining 10 roll pieces slightly and place over pepperoni mixture. Push edges down slightly to seal. Bake in 350°F (175°C) oven for 15 to 20 minutes. Makes 10.

1 pop-up: 153 Calories; 10.6 g Total Fat; 589 mg Sodium; 6 g Protein; 8 g Carbohydrate; trace Dietary Fiber

TUNA TURNOVERS

These little packets are a delicious variation of the more traditional sandwich.

Can of tuna, drained and flaked	$6\frac{1}{2}$ oz.	184 g
Large hard-boiled eggs, chopped	2	2
Chopped chives	2 tsp.	10 mL
Dill weed	$\frac{1}{8}$-$\frac{1}{4}$ tsp.	0.5-1 mL
Onion powder	$\frac{1}{4}$ tsp.	1 mL
Condensed cream of celery soup	$\frac{1}{2}$ x 10 oz.	$\frac{1}{2}$ x 284 mL
Jumbo refrigerator crescent-style rolls (4 per tube)	8 oz.	318 g

Put first 6 ingredients into medium bowl. Mix well. Makes $1\frac{1}{2}$ cups (375 mL) filling.

Separate crescent dough into 4 rectangles. Scoop generous $\frac{1}{3}$ cup (75 mL) tuna mixture onto each piece of dough. Moisten edges. Fold over and seal. Arrange on greased baking sheet. Bake in 375°F (190°C) oven for about 10 minutes until hot and browned. Makes 4.

1 turnover: 256 Calories; 11.1 g Total Fat; 865 mg Sodium; 20 g Protein; 18 g Carbohydrate; trace Dietary Fiber

---

Prior to chopping an onion, rub your hands with a bit of vinegar like you were putting on hand lotion. It will keep them from smelling like an onion.

TRENDY TACOS

A good do-it-yourself meal.

Lean ground chicken	1 lb.	454 g
Cooking oil	1 tbsp.	15 mL
Chili powder	1½ tsp.	7 mL
Salt	½ tsp.	2 mL
Pepper	⅛ tsp.	0.5 mL
Dried whole oregano	¼ tsp.	1 mL
Garlic powder	¼ tsp.	1 mL
Paprika	1 tsp.	5 mL
Taco shells	10	10
Medium tomatoes, diced	2	2
Shredded lettuce, lightly packed	1½ cups	375 mL
Onion slivers (optional)	⅓ cup	75 mL
Grated light medium or sharp Cheddar cheese	¾ cup	175 mL
Sliced pitted ripe olives (optional)	10	10
Non-fat sour cream	⅔ cup	150 mL

Scramble-fry chicken in cooking oil in frying pan until no longer pink. Drain.

Add next 6 ingredients. Mix well.

Spoon about 2 tbsp. (30 mL) chicken mixture into each taco shell. Divide remaining 6 ingredients, in layers, over chicken mixture. Makes 10.

1 taco: 141 Calories; 9.4 g Total Fat; 241 mg Sodium; 13 g Protein; 10 g Carbohydrate; 1 g Dietary Fiber

TACO DOG

A great twist to a great snack.

Wiener, halved lengthwise and fried	1	1
Taco shell	1	1
Chili con carne, heated	2 tbsp.	30 mL
Grated Monterey Jack cheese	1 tbsp.	15 mL
Shredded lettuce	2 tbsp.	30 mL
Diced tomato	1 tbsp.	15 mL
Grated Cheddar cheese (optional)	1 tbsp.	15 mL

Place hot fried wiener in taco shell. Add chili and Monterey Jack cheese on top. Heat in 350°F (175°C) oven to melt cheese.

Layer lettuce, tomato and Cheddar cheese over top. Serves 1.

1 serving: 236 Calories; 17.1 g Total Fat; 629 mg Sodium; 9 g Protein; 13 g Carbohydrate; 2 g Dietary Fiber

Pictured on page 89.

Place taco shells on a baking sheet and heat in oven for a few minutes to freshen their flavor.

CORNED HERO

Gooey to eat but makes an impressive sight.

French bread loaf (see Note)	1	1
Non-fat sour cream	¼ cup	60 mL
Light salad dressing (or mayonnaise)	2 tbsp.	30 mL
Chopped chives	1 tsp.	5 mL
Parsley flakes	1 tsp.	5 mL
Onion powder	⅛ tsp.	0.5 mL
Large tomato, sliced	1	1
Shaved corned beef	12 oz.	340 g
Process light Cheddar cheese slices	6	6

Slice bread in half horizontally. Toast in hot oven or under broiler.

Mix next 5 ingredients in small bowl. Spread on bottom half of loaf.

Layer tomato slices, corned beef and cheese over sour cream mixture. Broil to melt and slightly brown cheese. Place top half of bread over melted cheese. Cuts into 6 thick slices.

1 slice: 449 Calories; 18.6 g Total Fat; 1262 mg Sodium; 23 g Protein; 45 g Carbohydrate; 2 g Dietary Fiber

Note: If you prefer a thinner loaf, cut out a horizontal center slice and use for another purpose.

CORNED BEEF IN RYE

Ready in 15 minutes.

Oblong rye loaf (light or dark)	16 oz.	500 g
Dijon mustard	2 tbsp.	30 mL
Finely chopped cabbage, lightly packed	2 cups	500 mL
Light salad dressing (or mayonnaise)	⅓ cup	75 mL
Granulated sugar	1 tsp.	5 mL
Lemon juice	1 tbsp.	15 mL
Red apple (such as McIntosh), with peel, cored and finely diced	1	1
Shaved corned beef	8 oz.	225 g
Grated Swiss cheese	1 cup	250 mL

Cut 2 inch (5 cm) horizontal slice from top of bread loaf. Hollow out bottom of loaf with fork leaving about ½ inch (12 mm) shell. Spread mustard on cut side of bread top.

Combine cabbage, salad dressing, sugar, lemon juice and apple in medium bowl. Mix well.

Layer ⅓ of corned beef in bottom of bread shell. Top with ½ of cheese and ½ of cabbage mixture. Repeat with ⅓ of beef, remaining ½ of cheese, remaining ½ of cabbage mixture and top with remaining ⅓ of beef. Place top over beef. Press down. Wrap in plastic wrap. Chill. Cuts into six 2 inch (5 cm) slices.

1 slice: 289 Calories; 13.3 g Total Fat; 688 mg Sodium; 14 g Protein; 31 g Carbohydrate; 2 g Dietary Fiber

PITA SANDWICHES

This fantastic pocket bread lends itself to hot or cold fillings.

Margarine	4 tsp.	20 mL
Pita breads (6 inch, 15 cm, size), cut in half	2	2
Chicken Filling, page 61	⅔ cup	150 mL
Lettuce leaves	4	4
Light cottage cheese	½ cup	125 mL
Chopped green pepper	2 tbsp.	30 mL
Avocado slice, cut small	1	1
Lemon juice	1 tsp.	5 mL
Alfalfa sprouts (optional)		

Spread margarine on inside of each pita half.

Spread thin layer of filling inside each. Line with lettuce.

Mix cottage cheese and green pepper in small bowl. Spoon into pita.

Dip avocado into lemon juice, then push partly into cottage cheese mixture. Add a few alfalfa sprouts. Makes 4.

1 pita pocket: *296 Calories; 17.7 g Total Fat; 456 mg Sodium; 11 g Protein; 25 g Carbohydrate; 2 g Dietary Fiber*

PICKLY PITA POCKETS

A delicious crunch to it. Eat now or make ahead and cover and chill overnight.

Diced ham (or beef roast or salami)	1 cup	250 mL
Finely chopped dill pickle, blotted dry with paper towel	⅓ cup	75 mL
Light salad dressing (or mayonnaise)	2 tbsp.	30 mL
Prepared mustard	1 tsp.	5 mL
Pita breads (6 inch, 15 cm, size), cut in half	2	2

Combine ham, pickle, salad dressing and mustard in small bowl. Mix well. Makes about 1⅓ cups (325 mL) filling. Spoon filling into each pita half. Makes 4.

1 pita pocket: *156 Calories; 4.2 g Total Fat; 889 mg Sodium; 10 g Protein; 19 g Carbohydrate; trace Dietary Fiber*

1. Taco Dog, page 86
2. Grilled Raisin And Cheese, page 111
3. Peanut Butter Wrap, page 56
4. Bacon Cheese Roll-Up, page 57

Props Courtesy Of: Stokes

MEXI-BEEF PITAS

A great kids' lunch or after school snack. Make the filling ahead and keep on hand. Makes ten mini pita sandwiches.

Mini pita breads (3 inch, 7.5 cm, size)	10	10
Lean ground beef	1 lb.	454 g
Finely chopped onion	¹/₂ cup	125 mL
Can of pinto beans, drained	14 oz.	398 mL
Diced green pepper	¹/₂ cup	125 mL
Diced red pepper	¹/₄ cup	60 mL
Chili powder	2 tsp.	10 mL
Salt	1 tsp.	5 mL
Grated Monterey Jack cheese	³/₄ cup	175 mL

Place pita breads on ungreased baking sheet in 300°F (150°C) oven to warm.

Scramble-fry ground beef in non-stick frying pan until no longer pink. Drain.

Add next 6 ingredients. Mix well. Heat thoroughly for 2 to 3 minutes. Remove pita breads. Make slit in seam of each pita and open the "pocket." Spoon filling into warmed pitas.

Sprinkle with cheese. Place on ungreased baking sheet. Return to oven to melt cheese. Makes 10.

1 pita half: *190 Calories; 6.8 g Total Fat; 519 mg Sodium; 14 g Protein; 18 g Carbohydrate; trace Dietary Fiber*

SLICED TURKEY PITAS

The perfect lunch when you have leftover turkey.

Light spreadable cream cheese	3 tbsp.	50 mL
Pita bread (6 inch,15 cm, size), cut in half	1	1
Cranberry sauce	2 tbsp.	30 mL
Cooked turkey slices (about 3 oz., 85 g)	4	4
Shredded lettuce (or alfalfa sprouts), lightly packed	¹/₂ cup	125 mL

Spread cream cheese on inner top side of each pita half. Spread cranberry sauce on inner bottom side of each pocket. Place 1 slice of turkey in each pocket. Top each slice with lettuce. Place second slice of turkey over lettuce. Makes 2.

1 pita half: *204 Calories; 4.5 g Total Fat; 344 mg Sodium; 16 g Protein; 24 g Carbohydrate; trace Dietary Fiber*

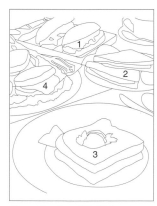

1. Scrambled Benedict, page 104
2. French Jelly Sandwich, page 103
3. Fruity Monte Cristo, page 105
4. Benedict Muffin, page 24

Props Courtesy Of: Stokes
                   X/S Wares

FRUITY CHICKEN PITAS

Store leftover filling in the refrigerator for two to three days.

Light salad dressing (or mayonnaise)	½ cup	125 mL
Raisins	⅓ cup	75 mL
Ground cinnamon	¼ tsp.	1 mL
Chopped walnuts (optional)	2 tbsp.	30 mL
Diced cooked chicken (or turkey)	1 cup	250 mL
Small red apple (with or without peel), cored and diced	1	1
Can of pineapple tidbits, well drained	8 oz.	227 mL
Crushed potato chips	1 cup	250 mL
Mini pita breads (3 inch, 7.5 cm, size)	10	10

Combine first 4 ingredients in small bowl.

Combine next 4 ingredients in medium bowl. Fold salad dressing mixture into chicken mixture until coated. Makes 2½ cups (625 mL) filling.

Carefully slit each pita bread open at 1 end. Fill each "pocket" with ¼ cup (60 mL) filling. Makes 10.

1 pita: 157 Calories; 5.8 g Total Fat; 186 mg Sodium; 7 g Protein; 20 g Carbohydrate; 1 g Dietary Fiber

Pictured on front cover.

GYRO SANDWICHES

Prepare and assemble in ten minutes.

GYRO SAUCE

Light salad dressing (or mayonnaise)	¾ cup	175 mL
Milk	¼ cup	60 mL
Garlic cloves, minced	2	2
Dried whole oregano	1 tsp.	5 mL
Pepper	¼ tsp.	1 mL
Pita breads (8 inch, 20 cm, size), cut in half	3	3
Thinly sliced cooked lean (or deli) beef	¾ lb.	340 g
Shredded lettuce, lightly packed	1 cup	250 mL
Chopped tomato	1 cup	250 mL
Thinly sliced red onion	½ cup	125 mL
Sliced pitted ripe olives	¼ cup	60 mL

Gyro Sauce: Combine first 5 ingredients in medium bowl. Chill.

Fill pita "pockets" with beef, lettuce, tomato, red onion and olives. Spoon Gyro Sauce into each filled pita half. Makes 6.

1 pita half: 287 Calories; 11.6 g Total Fat; 421 mg Sodium; 20 g Protein; 25 g Carbohydrate; 1 g Dietary Fiber

MEDITERRANEAN BEEF SALAD SANDWICHES

Make the salad the day before but remove from the marinade after two hours and chill overnight.

Cooked lean beef, cut into thin strips	$^1/_2$ lb.	225 g
Broccoli florets, blanched and put into ice water	1 cup	250 mL
Sliced cucumber, with peel	$^2/_3$ cup	150 mL
Sliced celery	$^2/_3$ cup	150 mL
Sliced red pepper	$^2/_3$ cup	150 mL
Halved pitted ripe olives	$^1/_4$ cup	60 mL
Pickled onions, sliced	10	10
Crumbled feta cheese	$^1/_2$ cup	125 mL
Freshly ground pepper, to taste		
Low-fat Italian dressing	$^1/_2$ cup	125 mL
Pita breads (8 inch, 20 cm, size), cut in half	6	6

Combine first 8 ingredients in medium bowl. Toss. Season with pepper. Add dressing. Toss well. Marinate in refrigerator for at least 1 hour to meld flavors.

Spoon salad into pita "pockets." Serve immediately. Makes 12.

1 pita half: 143 Calories; 2.5 g Total Fat; 510 mg Sodium; 9 g Protein; 21 g Carbohydrate; 1 g Dietary Fiber

Cucumbers taste best when stored at room temperature.

BEEF CALZONES

This could easily be one of your favorites. They are incredibly good.

Basic Pizza Crust dough, page 13	**1**	**1**
Beef stew meat, cut into ¹⁄₂ inch (12 mm) cubes	**³⁄₄ lb.**	**340 g**
Cooking oil	**2 tsp.**	**10 mL**
Water, to cover		
Salt	**¹⁄₂ tsp.**	**2 mL**
Pepper	**¹⁄₈ tsp.**	**0.5 mL**
Chopped onion	**¹⁄₂ cup**	**125 mL**
Commercial pizza sauce	**¹⁄₄ cup**	**60 mL**
Can of asparagus tips, drained	**12 oz.**	**341 mL**
Grated part-skim mozzarella cheese	**1¹⁄₃ cups**	**325 mL**

Prepare pizza dough. Divide into 4 equal balls. Cover. Let rest while preparing filling.

Brown beef in hot cooking oil in medium frying pan. Spoon into large saucepan.

Pour about 1 cup (250 mL) water into frying pan. Loosen all browned bits. Pour over beef in saucepan. Add water to cover, salt and pepper. Boil gently for 1 hour.

Add onion. Boil for 30 minutes. Strain, saving broth for soup if you like. Spread beef on large plate to cool.

Roll out 1 ball of dough on lightly floured surface into ¹⁄₈ inch (3 mm) thick circle. Spread ¹⁄₄ of pizza sauce over ¹⁄₂ of circle, keeping in from edge about 1 inch (2.5 cm). Layer ¹⁄₄ of beef mixture over sauce. Lay about 5 asparagus tips side by side over beef mixture. Sprinkle with ¹⁄₃ cup (75 mL) cheese. Dampen edge with water. Fold over and press to seal. Crimp edge with fork. Repeat, making 3 more. Place on greased baking sheet. Poke holes in tops. Bake on bottom rack in 425°F (220°C) oven for about 15 minutes. Makes 4.

1 calzone: 596 Calories; 23.2 g Total Fat; 1165 mg Sodium; 38 g Protein; 58 g Carbohydrate; 4 g Dietary Fiber

HAM AND CHEESE CALZONES

Very colorful filling.

Whole Wheat Pizza Crust dough, page 14	**1**	**1**
Cooking oil	**2 tsp.**	**10 mL**
Chopped green pepper	**½ cup**	**125 mL**
Chopped red pepper	**½ cup**	**125 mL**
Can of sliced mushrooms, drained	**10 oz.**	**284 mL**
Garlic powder	**¼ tsp.**	**1 mL**
Salt	**¼ tsp.**	**1 mL**
Pepper	**¹⁄₁₆ tsp.**	**0.5 mL**
Commercial pizza sauce	**¼ cup**	**60 mL**
Can of ham flakes, drained	**6½ oz.**	**184 g**
Grated Parmesan cheese	**4 tsp.**	**20 mL**
Grated Muenster cheese	**1 cup**	**250 mL**

Prepare pizza dough. Divide dough into 4 equal balls. Cover. Let rest while preparing filling.

Heat cooking oil in medium frying pan. Add green and red peppers. Sauté until tender-crisp. Remove from heat.

Add mushrooms, garlic powder, salt and pepper. Stir together.

Roll out 1 ball of dough on lightly floured surface into ⅛ inch (3 mm) thick circle. Spread ½ of circle with 1 tbsp. (15 mL) pizza sauce, keeping in from edge about 1 inch (2.5 cm). Spoon ¼ of mushroom mixture over top. Layer ¼ of ham over mushroom mixture. Sprinkle with 1 tsp. (5 mL) Parmesan cheese and ¼ cup (60 mL) Muenster cheese. Dampen edge with water. Fold over and press to seal. Crimp edge with fork. Repeat, making 3 more. Place on greased baking sheet. Poke holes in tops. Bake on bottom rack in 425°F (220°C) oven for about 15 minutes. Makes 4.

1 calzone: 569 Calories; 28.8 g Total Fat; 1425 mg Sodium; 25 g Protein; 55 g Carbohydrate; 7 g Dietary Fiber

MUFFULETTA

Pronounced muhf-ful-LEHT-tuh. This New Orleans specialty is a mixture of meat and cheese combined with an olive salad, all stuffed into a round loaf.

Chopped pimiento-stuffed olives	1 cup	250 mL
Jars of sliced pimiento (2 oz., 57 mL, each), drained	2	2
Chopped celery	½ cup	125 mL
Chopped green pepper	2 tbsp.	30 mL
Shredded carrot	2 tbsp.	30 mL
Garlic powder	¼ tsp.	1 mL
Ground oregano (optional)	¼ tsp.	1 mL
Olive (or cooking) oil	½ cup	125 mL
Red wine vinegar	½ cup	125 mL
Round Italian bread loaf (10 inches, 25 cm)	1	1
Genoa salami slices	4-6	4-6
Provolone cheese slices	4-6	4-6
Cooked ham slices	4-6	4-6
Swiss cheese slices	4-6	4-6

Mix first 9 ingredients in medium bowl. Marinate in refrigerator for several hours.

Slice loaf into 2 layers. Remove about ½ inch (12 mm) bread from both layers, leaving about a 1 inch (2.5 cm) edge. Brush layers with oil from olive mixture.

Spoon well-drained olive mixture over bottom half. Layer remaining 4 ingredients in order given. Place top half over olive mixture. Press down. Wrap tightly in plastic wrap. Chill, with a 1 or 2 lb. (454 or 900 g) item used as a weight on top, for at least 20 to 30 minutes. Cuts into 8 wedges.

1 wedge: 435 Calories; 25.6 g Total Fat; 1233 mg Sodium; 16 g Protein; 35 g Carbohydrate; 2 g Dietary Fiber

Pictured on front cover.

Quickly deodorize your cutting board by rubbing it with a paste made from water and baking soda. This paste can also be used to remove odors from your hands.

JELLY ROLL BREAD

You will find it difficult to wait until this is cool enough to slice.

Frozen bread loaf dough	1	1
Thin slices provolone cheese	6	6
Part-skim mozzarella cheese slices	6	6
Thin slices cooked ham	6	6
Grated Parmesan cheese	2-4 tbsp.	30-60 mL

Place dough in large bowl. Cover with damp tea towel. Let double in size. Work down. Roll into rectangular shape as thinly as you can, $\frac{1}{4}$ inch (6 mm) or less. Have 1 side measure about 12 inches (30 cm).

Cut provolone and mozzarella cheeses and ham into 4 strips per slice. This will allow for better expansion of dough. Arrange provolone from edge of short side of dough, leaving long sides uncovered $1\frac{1}{2}$ inches (3.8 cm) in from edge, also leaving at least 2 inches (5 cm) uncovered at other short end. Repeat with ham and mozzarella strips. Sprinkle with Parmesan cheese. Dampen all edges, except short side where cheese and ham are at edge. Roll from that edge. Press to seal. Squeeze ends together. Place, seam side down, in greased 9 × 5 × 3 inch (22 × 12.5 × 7.5 cm) loaf pan. Cover with waxed paper. Place tea towel over all. Allow to rise until doubled in size. Remove tea towel and waxed paper. Bake in 400°F (205°C) oven for about 25 minutes until dark brown. Cool for about 30 minutes. Cuts into 8 slices.

1 slice: 291 Calories; 11.4 g Total Fat; 897 mg Sodium; 18 g Protein; 28 g Carbohydrate; 1 g Dietary Fiber

QUICK BREAD "SANDWICH"

Cheese adds a nice flavor to the biscuit crust. Makes an impressive lunch. Just add a salad.

Biscuit mix	$1\frac{1}{2}$ cups	375 mL
Grated light sharp Cheddar cheese	1 cup	250 mL
Water	$\frac{3}{4}$ cup	175 mL
Dry mustard	1 tsp.	5 mL
Shaved ham (or other deli meat)	8 oz.	225 g
Grated light sharp Cheddar cheese	1 cup	250 mL
Green onions, sliced (optional)	2	2
Chopped green or red pepper	$\frac{1}{4}$ cup	60 mL

Combine biscuit mix, first amount of cheese, water and mustard in medium bowl. Mix well.

Spread $\frac{1}{2}$ of batter in greased 9 inch (22 cm) pie plate. Cover with ham, second amount of cheese, green onion and green pepper. Spread remaining $\frac{1}{2}$ of batter over top as best as you can. Bake, uncovered, in 350°F (175°C) oven for 25 to 30 minutes. Cuts into 6 wedges.

1 wedge: 317 Calories; 14.3 g Total Fat; 1231 mg Sodium; 20 g Protein; 25 g Carbohydrate; 1 g Dietary Fiber

SINGLE MUFFULETTA

Pronounced muhf-ful-LEHT-tuh. Make this New Orleans sandwich the night before to take for lunch the next day.

Italian-style crusty bun, split in half	1	1
Low-fat Italian dressing	1½ tbsp.	25 mL
Tomato slices	4	4
Part-skim mozzarella cheese slices	2	2
Cooked lean ham (or beef) slices (about 2 oz., 57 g)	2	2
Alfalfa sprouts (or lettuce)	⅓ cup	75 mL

Pull out bits of bread from soft center of both bun halves. Measure dressing into cup. Use pastry brush to spread about ½ tbsp. (7 mL) dressing on each half. Layer 2 slices of tomato, 1 slice of cheese and 1 slice of ham on bottom half of bun. Brush remaining dressing over ham. Top with alfalfa sprouts, remaining tomato slices, remaining cheese slice and remaining ham slice. Place top half of bun over ham. Press down. Makes 1.

1 sandwich: 365 Calories; 12.3 g Total Fat; 1663 mg Sodium; 27 g Protein; 36 g Carbohydrate; 2 g Dietary Fiber

CORN DOGGIES

Make these the night before and simply reheat for lunch. These also freeze well.

Envelope pie crust mix (9½ oz., 270 g)	1	1
Yellow cornmeal	⅓ cup	75 mL
Chili powder	1 tsp.	5 mL
Cold water, approximately	6 tbsp.	100 mL
All-purpose flour, as needed to prevent sticking when rolling		
Wieners	8	8
Large egg, fork-beaten	1	1

Empty pie crust mix into medium bowl. Stir in cornmeal and chili powder. Slowly add cold water, 1 tbsp. (15 mL) at a time, stirring with fork after each addition. Dough should start to pull away from sides of bowl and form a ball. Divide ball in half. Roll each half into 5 × 12 inch (12.5 × 30 cm) rectangle on lightly floured surface. Cut each rectangle crosswise into 4 equal rectangles, for a total of 8.

Place 1 wiener lengthwise across each rectangle. Brush 1 long edge of each rectangle with egg. Bring both long edges up over wiener and press together to seal. Place, seam side down, on ungreased baking sheet. Brush each surface with remaining egg. Bake in 450°F (230°C) oven for 12 minutes until crisp and golden. Makes 8.

1 doggie: 332 Calories; 22.8 g Total Fat; 665 mg Sodium; 8 g Protein; 23 g Carbohydrate; trace Dietary Fiber

Pictured on page 35.

FALAFELS

Make medium feh-LAH-fehl patties or balls to stuff a pita or make small balls for an appetizer.

Can of chickpeas (garbanzo beans), drained	**19 oz.**	**540 mL**
Chopped onion	**¾ cup**	**175 mL**
Ground cumin	**¾ tsp.**	**4 mL**
Garlic powder	**½ tsp.**	**2 mL**
Parsley flakes	**½ tsp.**	**2 mL**
Baking powder	**½ tsp.**	**2 mL**
Salt	**¾ tsp.**	**4 mL**
Pepper	**¼ tsp.**	**1 mL**
Ground coriander	**½ tsp.**	**2 mL**
Turmeric	**⅛ tsp.**	**0.5 mL**
Fine dry bread crumbs	**1 cup**	**250 mL**
Large eggs	**2**	**2**
Cooking oil, for deep-frying		
Pita breads	**11**	**11**

Run chickpeas and onion through food grinder or food processor. Place in large bowl.

Add next 10 ingredients. Mix well. Shape into 1 inch (2.5 cm) balls. Leave balls round or flatten into patties.

Lower balls or patties on slotted spoon into hot 375°F (190°C) cooking oil. Cook for about 45 seconds until desired shade of brown. Remove with slotted spoon to dish lined with paper towel.

Cut pitas in half. Stuff 4 balls or flattened patties in each. Makes 44 falafels, enough for 11 pitas.

1 pita plus 4 falafels: 342 Calories; 10.1 g Total Fat; 482 mg Sodium; 11 g Protein; 51 g Carbohydrate; 2 g Dietary Fiber

FALAFEL APPETIZERS: Shape into ¾ inch (2 cm) balls. Serve hot with cocktail picks on the side with tahini sauce for dipping. Makes about 65.

MAIN COURSE FALAFELS: Shape into 1½ inch (3.8 cm) balls to serve for a main course. Serve with tahini sauce. Makes about 22.

Another use for chickpeas (garbanzo beans) is to mix cooked or canned, drained, chickpeas with seasoned whole wheat flour and crushed garlic. Fry in a little margarine and cooking oil on high heat until crisp and golden. Use as a dip with deep-fried pita sections.

Submarines

Get ready to dive right into these wonderful recipes for submarine sandwiches. Make them long or short, layer them high or toast them hot. Have fun with Basic Sub, page 101, and get the kids involved. Serve Hero Sandwich, page 100, to the delight of everyone this weekend. That's the beauty of a submarine sandwich—they're made-to-order!

HERO SANDWICH

You will be a hero if you can finish this! You will be an even bigger hero if you share!

Submarine bun (12 inch, 30 cm), split	1	1
Light salad dressing (or mayonnaise)	1 tbsp.	15 mL
Prepared mustard	2 tsp.	10 mL
Thin slices salami (about 1½ oz., 42 g)	6	6
Thinly shaved deli ham (or chicken or turkey)	1½ oz.	42 g
Medium tomato, sliced	1	1
Part-skim mozzarella (or Monterey Jack) cheese, thinly sliced	2 oz.	57 g
Shredded lettuce (or mixed sprouts), lightly packed	½ cup	125 mL
Salt, sprinkle		
Pepper, sprinkle		

Cut submarine bun in half horizontally on cutting board. Pull out bits of bread from soft center of top and bottom halves, making a shallow hollow. Spread salad dressing on each half. Spread mustard on bottom half.

Layer next 4 ingredients on top of mustard-topped half. Top with lettuce. Sprinkle with salt and pepper. Place top half onto filled bottom half. Press down slightly. Cut in half on cutting board. Makes 1.

1 sub: 747 Calories; 31.3 g Total Fat; 2204 mg Sodium; 40 g Protein; 76 g Carbohydrate; 5 g Dietary Fiber

Pictured on page 107.

CHICKEN SUB

Roast a large enough chicken to have lots left over for sandwiches or roast some for sandwiches alone.

Margarine	1 tbsp.	15 mL
Submarine bun (8 inch, 20 cm), split	1	1
Spinach leaves (or romaine lettuce)	4-6	4-6
Sliced cooked chicken	3 oz.	85 g
Salt, sprinkle		
Pepper, sprinkle		
Provolone (or Swiss) cheese slice	1	1
Salami slices	4	4
Green pepper rings	4	4
Light salad dressing (or mayonnaise)	1 tbsp.	15 mL

Spread margarine on both halves of bun. Layer next 7 ingredients in order given on bottom half. This makes a neater job if bottom is hollowed out a bit first.

Spread salad dressing on top half of bun. Place over green pepper rings. Makes 1.

1 sub: 822 Calories; 45.4 g Total Fat; 1833 mg Sodium; 51 g Protein; 50 g Carbohydrate; 3 g Dietary Fiber

BASIC SUB

This popular sandwich lends itself to creativity. Use beef, chicken, deli meats and even hot cooked meats.

Margarine	1 tbsp.	15 mL
Submarine bun (8 inch, 20 cm), split	1	1
Part-skim mozzarella cheese slices	2	2
Shredded lettuce, lightly packed	¼ cup	60 mL
Cooked ham slices	2	2
Medium tomato, sliced	1	1
Salt, sprinkle		
Pepper, sprinkle		
Light salad dressing (or mayonnaise)	2 tbsp.	30 mL

Spread margarine on both halves of bun. Layer cheese, lettuce, ham and tomato on bottom half. Sprinkle with salt and pepper. Spread top half of bun with salad dressing. Place over tomato. Makes 1.

1 sub: 657 Calories; 34.4 g Total Fat; 2016 mg Sodium; 32 g Protein; 55 g Carbohydrate; 3 g Dietary Fiber

Prepackaged salad greens are great time-savers when making sandwiches in a hurry.

SUPER SAUSAGE SUBS

These will freeze well. Simply thaw before heating or pop in your lunch bag in the morning; by noon, the sub is well thawed. Heat in the microwave for one minute. A great lunch!

Ground sausage meat	1 lb.	454 g
Medium green pepper, cut into slivers	1	1
Medium onion, sliced	1	1
Pepper	$\frac{1}{8}$ tsp.	0.5 mL
Paprika	$\frac{1}{2}$ tsp.	2 mL
Cayenne pepper, sprinkle		
Meatless spaghetti sauce	1 cup	250 mL
Submarine buns (10 inch, 25 cm), split	4	4
Grated light Cheddar (or part-skim mozzarella) cheese	1 cup	250 mL

Scramble-fry sausage meat in frying pan for 5 minutes. Drain. Add green pepper, onion, pepper, paprika and cayenne pepper. Scramble-fry for 5 minutes until vegetables are tender-crisp and sausage is no longer pink. Stir in spaghetti sauce. Remove from heat. Makes 3 cups (750 mL) filling.

Pull out bits of bread from soft center of top and bottom halves of buns, making shallow hollow. Spoon filling into hollows. Top each with $\frac{1}{4}$ cup (60 mL) cheese. Place top halves of buns over cheese. Makes 4.

1 sub: 643 Calories; 31.5 g Total Fat; 1479 mg Sodium; 24 g Protein; 65 g Carbohydrate; 4 g Dietary Fiber

CHILI BOATS

Chili served the trendy way.

Medium onion, chopped	1	1
Lean ground beef	1 lb.	454 g
Margarine	2 tsp.	10 mL
Tomato paste	$5\frac{1}{2}$ oz.	156 mL
Water	1 cup	250 mL
Chili powder	2 tsp.	10 mL
Salt	1 tsp.	5 mL
Pepper	$\frac{1}{4}$ tsp.	1 mL
Submarine buns (8 inch, 20 cm), split	6	6

Scramble-fry onion and ground beef in margarine in frying pan until beef is no longer pink.

Add next 5 ingredients. Simmer for 5 minutes. Makes about 3 cups (750 mL).

Cut thin layer from top of bun which can be used as a lid. Hollow out bun. Fill with about $\frac{1}{2}$ cup (125 mL) filling. Replace bun lid if desired. Makes 6.

1 sub: 448 Calories; 17.6 g Total Fat; 950 mg Sodium; 22 g Protein; 50 g Carbohydrate; 3 g Dietary Fiber

Toasted/Grilled Sandwiches

toasted sandwich grabs everyone's attention the minute they step into the kitchen. Try Bacon And Egg Sandwich, page 109, when lunch needs to be quick and warm, or Lasagne Sandwich, page 111, after a day outdoors in the colder weather. Don't be surprised if your guests request one or more of these recipes to take back to their kitchens.

FRENCH JELLY SANDWICH

Make for Mom and Dad on Saturday morning. Serve with syrup or sprinkle with icing sugar.

Jelly (or jam), your favorite	2 tbsp.	30 mL
White (or whole wheat) bread slices	2	2
Large egg	1	1
Milk	1 tbsp.	15 mL
Granulated sugar	1 tsp.	5 mL
Salt, sprinkle		
Vanilla	1/4 tsp.	1 mL
Margarine	1 tsp.	5 mL

Spread jelly on 1 bread slice. Place second slice over jelly. Press down.

Beat egg with fork in pie plate. Add milk, sugar, salt and vanilla. Beat with fork until blended. Dip both sides of jelly sandwich into egg mixture.

Melt margarine in frying pan until bubbling. Place jelly sandwich in margarine. Cook until golden, turning sandwich over once to brown other side. Cook until golden. Makes 1.

1 sandwich: 396 Calories; 10.9 g Total Fat; 405 mg Sodium; 12 g Protein; 62 g Carbohydrate; 1 g Dietary Fiber

Pictured on page 90.

SCRAMBLED BENEDICT

A cross between a Denver Sandwich and Eggs Benedict. A hearty snack.

Finely chopped onion	1 tbsp.	15 mL
Margarine	1 tsp.	5 mL
Large egg	1	1
Water	1 tbsp.	15 mL
Cooked ham slice (or bacon, cooked crisp)	1	1
Medium tomato slice	1	1
Shredded lettuce	2 tbsp.	30 mL
English muffin, split and toasted	1	1

Sauté onion in margarine in frying pan until clear and soft.

Add egg and water. Scramble-fry.

Layer ham, tomato and lettuce on bottom half of toasted muffin. Top with scrambled egg mixture. Place second half of muffin over egg. Makes 1.

1 muffin half: 307 Calories; 12.2 g Total Fat; 790 mg Sodium; 19 g Protein; 30 g Carbohydrate; 1 g Dietary Fiber

Pictured on page 90.

REUBEN SANDWICH

Served hot, this is a favorite.

Thin slices corned beef	2-4	2-4
Sauerkraut, drained and rinsed	2 tbsp.	30 mL
Part-skim mozzarella cheese slice	1	1
Rye (or pumpernickel) bread slices	2	2
Margarine	2 tsp.	10 mL

Layer corned beef, sauerkraut and cheese on 1 bread slice. Place second slice over cheese. Butter outside of sandwich. Grill. Makes 1.

1 sandwich: 427 Calories; 22.5 g Total Fat; 1341 mg Sodium; 22 g Protein; 36 g Carbohydrate; 4 g Dietary Fiber

Pictured on page 107.

Variation: Spread 1 slice bread with Thousand Island salad dressing before adding filling.

CHICKEN REUBEN

Just filled with good taste.

Light salad dressing (or mayonnaise)	1 tbsp.	15 mL
Chili sauce	1 tsp.	5 mL
Sweet pickle relish	¾ tsp.	4 mL
Onion powder, just a pinch		
Pumpernickel (or rye) bread slices	2	2
Thin slices cooked chicken	3	3
Sauerkraut, drained and rinsed	3 tbsp.	50 mL
Swiss (or part-skim mozzarella) cheese slice	1	1

Mix first 4 ingredients well in small bowl.

Spread ½ of salad dressing mixture over each bread slice. On 1 slice, layer chicken, sauerkraut and cheese. Place second slice over cheese. Fry in greased frying pan, browning both sides. Makes 1.

1 sandwich: 446 Calories; 13.6 g Total Fat; 902 mg Sodium; 40 g Protein; 41 g Carbohydrate; 5 g Dietary Fiber

FRUITY MONTE CRISTO

An unusual sandwich that could even be served for breakfast.

Can of chicken flakes, drained	6½ oz.	184 g
Coarsely chopped raisins	2 tbsp.	30 mL
Crushed pineapple, drained	¼ cup	60 mL
Light salad dressing (or mayonnaise)	1 tbsp.	15 mL
Margarine	2½ tbsp.	37 mL
White (or whole wheat) bread slices	8	8
Large eggs, fork-beaten	2	2
Water	¼ cup	60 mL
Icing (confectioner's) sugar, sprinkle		

Stir first 4 ingredients well in small bowl.

Spread margarine on bread slices. Divide and spread chicken mixture on 4 slices. Cover with remaining 4 slices.

Stir beaten eggs and water in shallow bowl. Dip sandwiches into egg mixture, coating both sides. Brown both sides in well-greased frying pan for about 3 minutes per side. Cut each sandwich in half and put onto individual plates.

Sift icing sugar over top. Makes 4.

1 sandwich: 352 Calories; 15.9 g Total Fat; 643 mg Sodium; 18 g Protein; 34 g Carbohydrate; 1 g Dietary Fiber

Pictured on page 90.

TOAST CUPS

Fill these with any sandwich filling.

Margarine	¼ cup	60 mL
White (or whole wheat) bread slices, crusts removed	12	12

Spread margarine on bread slices. Press each slice, buttered side down, into ungreased muffin cup. Bake in 350°F (175°C) oven for 15 to 20 minutes until crisp and toasted. Makes 12.

1 toast cup: 167 Calories; 7.3 g Total Fat; 293 mg Sodium; 4 g Protein; 21 g Carbohydrate; 1 g Dietary Fiber

Pictured on page 18.

GARLIC TOAST CUPS: Stir ¼ tsp. (1 mL) garlic powder into margarine before spreading on bread slices.

Denver Sandwich

You will find this gratifying any time of day. Also called Western. Double quantity for a thick sandwich.

Large egg	1	1
Water (or milk)	1 tbsp.	15 mL
Chopped cooked ham	2 tbsp.	30 mL
Finely chopped onion	1 tbsp.	15 mL
Finely chopped green pepper	1 tbsp.	15 mL
Salt, sprinkle		
Pepper, sprinkle		
Margarine	2 tsp.	10 mL
White (or whole wheat) bread slices, toasted	2	2

Beat egg and water in medium bowl. Add ham, onion, green pepper, salt and pepper. Pour slowly into hot, well-greased frying pan. It will start to cook and won't spread too much. As it cooks, keep drawing to center to keep bread-shape. Brown lightly. Turn to brown other side.

Spread margarine on toast. Place filling on 1 slice of toast. Cover with remaining slice. Cut and serve hot. Makes 1.

1 sandwich: 325 Calories; 15.5 g Total Fat; 735 mg Sodium; 15 g Protein; 30 g Carbohydrate; 1 g Dietary Fiber

Beef Slaw Sandwiches

A sandwich and salad all in one.

Finely shredded cabbage, lightly packed	1 cup	250 mL
Finely shredded carrot	¼ cup	60 mL
Low-fat coleslaw dressing	1 tbsp.	15 mL
Prepared horseradish	½ tsp.	2 mL
Margarine	2½ tbsp.	37 mL
White (or whole wheat) bread slices, toasted	8	8
Process light Cheddar cheese slices	4	4
Cooked roast beef slices	4	4
Salt, sprinkle		
Pepper, sprinkle		

Mix first 4 ingredients in small bowl. Set aside.

Spread margarine on toast slices. Layer cheese and beef on 4 slices. Sprinkle with salt and pepper. Top with cabbage mixture. Cover with remaining 4 toast slices. Makes 4.

1 sandwich: 346 Calories; 15.3 g Total Fat; 580 mg Sodium; 19 g Protein; 32 g Carbohydrate; 2 g Dietary Fiber

1. Hero Sandwich, page 100
2. Reuben Sandwich, page 104
3. Bean Burgers, page 20

Props Courtesy Of: The Bay

BACON AND EGG SANDWICH

A meal in a sandwich. Good without the egg too.

Margarine	2 tsp.	10 mL
Toast slices	2	2
Large egg, fried firm	1	1
Salt, sprinkle		
Pepper, sprinkle		
Bacon slices, cooked crisp, cut in half	2	2
Ketchup (optional)		

Spread margarine on toast slices. Layer egg, salt, pepper and bacon on 1 slice. Top with ketchup. Place second slice over bacon. Serve hot. Makes 1.

1 sandwich: 366 Calories; 20.6 g Total Fat; 651 mg Sodium; 15 g Protein; 29 g Carbohydrate; 1 g Dietary Fiber

BACON AND TOMATO SANDWICH: Omit egg. Add sliced tomato. Sprinkle with salt and pepper. A popular sandwich.

AVOCADO BACON SNACK: Add sliced avocado to Bacon And Tomato Sandwich.

PEANUT BUTTER AND BACON SANDWICH

Make this sandwich and wrap it with plastic wrap and take it to school. Heat in the microwave oven when ready for lunch.

Peanut butter (smooth or crunchy)	1½ tbsp.	25 mL
White (or whole wheat) bread slices, toasted	2	2
Bacon slices, cooked crisp	2	2
Part-skim mozzarella cheese slice	1	1
Margarine	1½ tsp.	7 mL

Spread peanut butter on 1 slice of toast. Break each slice of bacon into 2 pieces. Lay all 4 pieces over peanut butter. Top with cheese slice. Spread margarine on second slice of toast. Place over cheese. Makes 1.

1 sandwich: 485 Calories; 30.3 g Total Fat; 787 mg Sodium; 21 g Protein; 34 g Carbohydrate; 2 g Dietary Fiber

1. Egg Fajitas, page 116
2. Vegetable Roll, page 58

Props Courtesy Of: Stokes
The Bay

Toasted Ham And Cheese

Always popular, with warm cheese oozing from the sandwich.

Prepared mustard	1 tsp.	5 mL
Whole wheat (or white) bread slices	2	2
Thin slice lean ham (1 oz., 28 g)	1	1
Part-skim mozzarella cheese slice	1	1
Sweet pickle relish	1½ tsp.	7 mL
Margarine	2 tsp.	10 mL

Spread mustard on 1 bread slice. Lay ham and cheese over mustard. Spread relish on second bread slice. Place over cheese.

Spread margarine on outside of both slices. Brown on both sides in frying pan. Cut in half diagonally. Makes 1.

1 sandwich: 307 Calories; 11 g Total Fat; 982 mg Sodium; 17 g Protein; 32 g Carbohydrate; 4 g Dietary Fiber

Mozzarella Sandwich

Another great standby.

Part-skim mozzarella cheese slice	1	1
Medium tomato slices	3	3
Salt, sprinkle		
Pepper, sprinkle		
Dried sweet basil, sprinkle		
Lean cooked ham slice	1	1
Lettuce, to cover		
White (or whole wheat) bread slices	2	2
Margarine	2 tsp.	10 mL

Layer first 7 ingredients on 1 bread slice in order given. Place second bread slice over lettuce.

Spread margarine on outside of both slices. Brown on both sides in frying pan. Makes 1.

1 sandwich: 331 Calories; 14.8 g Total Fat; 999 mg Sodium; 18 g Protein; 31 g Carbohydrate; 2 g Dietary Fiber

Tuna Sandwiches

A good combination of flavors from the different cheeses and tomato.

Margarine	2½ tbsp.	37 mL
White (or whole wheat) bread slices, toasted	8	8
Can of tuna, drained and flaked	6½ oz.	184 g
Part-skim mozzarella cheese slices	4	4
Large tomato slices	4	4
Gruyère cheese slices	4	4
Alfalfa sprouts, large handful (optional)		

Spread margarine on 1 side of toast slices. Divide and spread tuna on 4 slices. Layer mozzarella cheese, tomato and Gruyère cheese over tuna. Broil on baking sheet until cheese is melted.

Layer alfalfa sprouts over cheese. Place remaining 4 toast slices over sprouts. Cut each sandwich in half. Makes 4.

1 sandwich: 362 Calories; 17.7 g Total Fat; 543 mg Sodium; 25 g Protein; 25 g Carbohydrate; 1 g Dietary Fiber

GRILLED RAISIN AND CHEESE

Raisin bread adds lots of flavor to this classic!

Process cheese slices (your favorite)	2	2
Raisin bread slices	2	2
Margarine	2 tsp.	10 mL

Overlap cheese slices on 1 bread slice. Place second slice over cheese. Spread margarine on outside of both slices. Brown both sides in frying pan. Cut in half. Makes 1.

1 sandwich: 355 Calories; 22 g Total Fat; 881 mg Sodium; 13 g Protein; 28 g Carbohydrate; 2 g Dietary Fiber

Pictured on page 89.

LASAGNE SANDWICH

This is grilled and is indeed reminiscent of lasagne.

Part-skim mozzarella cheese slice	1	1
White (or whole wheat) bread slices	2	2
Non-fat sour cream	1 tbsp.	15 mL
Onion flakes, crushed	1 tsp.	5 mL
Ground oregano	$\frac{1}{8}$ tsp.	0.5 mL
Medium tomato slices	3	3
Bacon slices, cooked crisp, cut in half	2	2
Margarine	2 tsp.	10 mL

Put cheese onto 1 bread slice.

Mix sour cream, onion flakes and oregano in small bowl. Spread over cheese slice.

Arrange tomato slices over sour cream mixture. Put bacon over tomato. Place second slice over bacon.

Spread margarine on outside of both slices. Brown both sides in frying pan. Makes 1.

1 sandwich: 385 Calories; 22.5 g Total Fat; 982 mg Sodium; 14 g Protein; 32 g Carbohydrate; 1 g Dietary Fiber

Pictured on page 35.

PINEAPPLE GRILLED CHEESE

Quite a surprise inside!

Crushed pineapple, well drained	2 tbsp.	30 mL
Finely chopped pecans (optional)	2 tsp.	10 mL
Process cheese slices	2	2
White (or whole wheat) bread slices	2	2
Margarine	2 tsp.	10 mL

Combine pineapple and pecans in cup. Stir.

Put 1 cheese slice on 1 slice of bread. Spread pineapple mixture on cheese. Put second cheese slice over pineapple. Place second bread slice on top of cheese. Spread margarine on outside of both bread slices. Brown on both sides in frying pan. Makes 1.

1 sandwich: 385 Calories; 22.5 g Total Fat; 982 mg Sodium; 14 g Protein; 32 g Carbohydrate; 1 g Dietary Fiber

Wraps

Ready to try something different? Well, wrap it all up with these inviting recipes. Try a variety of wrap breads to add flavor and color, and make them as filling or as light as you want.

Trying to decide what your favorite lunchtime meal is? Maybe you'll discover it right here.

That's a wrap everyone!

SALAD ENVELOPES

A salad you can eat with your fingers.

Medium tomato	1	1
Grated carrot	¼ cup	60 mL
Green onion, thinly sliced	1	1
Thinly sliced green, red or yellow pepper	¼ cup	60 mL
Grated light Cheddar cheese	1 cup	250 mL
Low-fat creamy dressing (your favorite)	2 tbsp.	30 mL
Shredded iceberg lettuce, lightly packed	⅔ cup	150 mL
White (or whole wheat) flour tortillas (10 inch, 25 cm, size)	2	2

Cut tomato in half. Gently squeeze over paper towel to remove seeds. Discard seeds and juice. Dice tomato into 1 inch (2.5 cm) chunks.

Combine tomato, carrot, green onion, green pepper and cheese in medium bowl. Stir.

Add dressing. Toss mixture together. Spread ½ of lettuce down middle of each tortilla. Leave some tortilla uncovered at 1 end to fold up envelope-style. Spread ½ of veggie mixture over lettuce. Fold bottom of tortilla up and then fold each side in. Leave top open. Wrap in paper towels to eat. Makes 2.

1 envelope: 460 Calories; 22.8 g Total Fat; 1053 mg Sodium; 20 g Protein; 42 g Carbohydrate; 3 g Dietary Fiber

Pictured on front cover.

Mexican Stir-Fry Sandwiches

Lots of color! Great taste! Change the spiciness according to your preference.

Cooking oil	1 tsp.	5 mL
Boneless, skinless chicken breast half (about 4 oz., 113 g), slivered	1	1
Garlic powder	⅛ tsp.	0.5 mL
Salt	⅛ tsp.	0.5 mL
Pepper	¹/₁₆ tsp.	0.5 mL
Small red (or other mild) onion, thinly sliced	½	½
Medium green, red or yellow pepper, slivered	½	½
Salsa (mild, medium or hot)	⅓ cup	75 mL
White (or whole wheat) flour tortillas (8 inch, 20 cm, size)	3	3

Heat cooking oil in frying pan over medium-high heat. Stir-fry chicken for 2 minutes.

Add garlic powder, salt and pepper. Stir-fry for 2 minutes.

Add red onion and green pepper to chicken. Stir-fry for 3 minutes. Add salsa. Stir-fry for 2 minutes until vegetables are tender-crisp. Remove frying pan to hot pad. Makes 2 cups (500 mL) filling.

Divide filling among tortillas. Fold bottom edge of tortilla up to center, over chicken mixture. Fold left side over center and then fold right side over center, overlapping left side. Makes 3.

1 sandwich: 219 Calories; 7.3 g Total Fat; 905 mg Sodium; 12 g Protein; 26 g Carbohydrate; 2 g Dietary Fiber

When stir-frying, cook vegetables until tender-crisp and still brightly colored.

OVEN BURRITOS

Several breakfast ingredients, spiced and rolled in tortillas. Serve with sour cream and salsa.

Bacon slices, cut into ½ inch (12 mm) pieces	8	8
Cooking oil	2 tsp.	10 mL
Sliced fresh mushrooms	1 cup	250 mL
Finely chopped green pepper	½ cup	125 mL
Chopped onion	½ cup	125 mL
Large eggs	8	8
Water (or milk)	3 tbsp.	50 mL
Grated Monterey Jack cheese	¼ cup	60 mL
Salsa (mild or medium)	3 tbsp.	50 mL
Chopped chives	1 tbsp.	15 mL
Garlic powder	¼ tsp.	1 mL
Flour tortillas (9 inch, 22 cm, size)	4	4
Grated medium Cheddar cheese	2 tbsp.	30 mL
Grated Monterey Jack cheese	2 tbsp.	30 mL

Cook bacon pieces in frying pan until almost crisp. Drain on paper towel.

Heat cooking oil in frying pan. Add mushrooms, green pepper and onion. Sauté until soft. Add bacon. Keep warm.

Beat eggs in medium bowl. Add water, first amount of Monterey Jack cheese, salsa, chives and garlic powder. Beat to mix. Pour into non-stick frying pan sprayed with no-stick cooking spray. Cook on medium-low, stirring often, until eggs are partially set. Add mushroom mixture. Cover. Cook until set. Cut into pieces to fill tortillas.

Divide mixture and place down center of each tortilla. Roll. Place, seam side down, in greased 9 x 9 inch (22 x 22 cm) pan.

Sprinkle with Cheddar cheese and second amount of Monterey Jack cheese. Bake in 350°F (175°C) oven for 20 to 30 minutes until heated through. Makes 4.

1 burrito: 445 Calories; 24 g Total Fat; 631 mg Sodium; 25 g Protein; 39 g Carbohydrate; 1 g Dietary Fiber

Instead of using a knife to chop bacon, try snipping it with a pair of kitchen scissors while it is partially frozen.

Speedy Fajitas

Only 20 minutes from start to finish when you buy precut stir-fry strips.

Lime juice	1 tbsp.	15 mL
Chili powder	1 tbsp.	15 mL
Dried whole oregano	1 tsp.	5 mL
Garlic powder	½ tsp.	2 mL
Freshly ground pepper, to taste		
Beef stir-fry strips	1 lb.	454 g
Sliced fresh mushrooms	2 cups	500 mL
Medium green or red pepper, cut into strips	1	1
Green onions, cut into 1 inch (2.5 cm) pieces	4	4
Cooking oil	2 tsp.	10 mL
Flour tortillas (10 inch, 25 cm, size)	8	8
Salsa (mild, medium or hot)	½ cup	125 mL

Mix first 5 ingredients in medium bowl. Add beef strips and stir to coat. Set aside.

Sauté mushrooms, green pepper strips and green onion in cooking oil in non-stick frying pan for 2 to 3 minutes. Remove vegetables to large bowl.

Wrap tortillas in damp tea towel and warm in oven.

Stir-fry beef strips, along with marinade, in non-stick frying pan for 5 minutes or until browned. Add beef mixture to vegetable mixture. Divide among 8 warmed tortillas (½ cup, 125 mL, filling per tortilla). Put 1 tbsp. (15 mL) salsa onto each tortilla. Fold up bottom and then fold in 2 sides, envelope-style, leaving top open. Makes 8.

1 fajita: 242 Calories; 6.2 g Total Fat, 18 g Protein; 29 g Carbohydrate; 2 g Dietary Fiber

Barbecued Fajitas

Keep beef more rare than well done as flank steak is more tender that way. Set out bowls of chopped tomato, hot pepper slivers, sliced green onion and shredded lettuce for guests to choose their own toppings.

Lime juice	¼ cup	60 mL
Olive oil	1 tbsp.	15 mL
Dried whole oregano	1 tbsp.	15 mL
Dried crushed chilies	½ tsp.	2 mL
Salt	¼ tsp.	1 mL
Freshly ground pepper	⅛ tsp.	0.5 mL
Garlic cloves, crushed	2	2
Flank steak	1½ lbs.	680 g
Flour tortillas (8 inch, 20 cm, size)	8	8

Combine first 7 ingredients in small bowl. Pour over steak in shallow dish or sealable plastic bag. Turn to coat. Cover or seal. Marinate in refrigerator overnight, turning several times. Remove steak, discarding marinade. Barbecue over medium heat for 5 to 7 minutes per side for medium or until desired doneness. Cut steak diagonally across grain into thin slices.

Wrap tortillas in foil. Heat in 350°F (175°C) oven for 8 to 10 minutes until warmed but still soft. Fill with sliced steak and selected garnishes. Makes 8.

1 fajita: 265 Calories; 7.2 g Total Fat; 214 mg Sodium; 23 g Protein; 25 g Carbohydrate; trace Dietary Fiber

EGG FAJITAS

*Everyone can roll their own or fillings can be
divided among tortillas and all rolled before the
meal.*

Large onion, halved lengthwise and thinly sliced	1	1
Medium green pepper, slivered	1	1
Medium yellow pepper, slivered	1	1
Water	⅓ cup	75 mL
Can of beans in tomato sauce (or refried beans)	14 oz.	398 mL
Grated Monterey Jack cheese	1½ cups	375 mL
Shredded lettuce, lightly packed	1½ cups	375 mL
Medium tomatoes, diced	2	2
Large eggs	9	9
Water	3 tbsp.	50 mL
Chili powder	¼ tsp.	1 mL
Cayenne pepper	⅛ tsp.	0.5 mL
Salt, sprinkle		
Pepper, sprinkle		
Flour tortillas (9 inch, 22 cm, size)	6	6
Salsa (mild, medium or hot)	⅓ cup	75 mL

Simmer onion and peppers in first amount of water
in large saucepan until soft. Keep warm. Add a bit
more water, if necessary, to keep from burning.

Heat beans in small saucepan until hot.

Arrange cheese, lettuce and tomato in separate
bowls.

Combine next 6 ingredients in medium bowl. Beat
lightly. Pour into greased, heated frying pan. Cook
and stir until eggs are set. Turn into separate bowl.

Wrap tortillas in foil. Heat in 350°F (175°C) oven
for 8 to 10 minutes until warmed but still soft.
Spoon eggs, beans, onion mixture, cheese,
lettuce, tomato and salsa into tortillas. Roll up,
folding in 1 end as you roll. Makes 6.

*1 fajita: 433 Calories; 17.7 g Total Fat; 896 mg Sodium;
25 g Protein; 56 g Carbohydrate; 8 g Dietary Fiber*

Pictured on page 108.

*To keep cheese from drying out, wrap in a cloth
dampened with vinegar.*

Meatless Fajitas

This meatless recipe uses tofu wieners for a fajita with a sweet and sour taste. Serve bowls of sour cream, guacamole, salsa and grated cheese and have people create their own.

Cooking oil	1 tbsp.	15 mL
Thinly sliced onion	1½ cups	375 mL
Large green pepper, thinly sliced into long matchsticks	1	1
Medium potatoes, cut as for french fries	2	2
Boiling water, to cover		
Flour tortillas (8 inch, 20 cm, size)	6	6
Can of diced green chilies, drained	4 oz.	114 mL
White vinegar	2 tbsp.	30 mL
Liquid honey	2 tsp.	10 mL
Garlic powder	½ tsp.	2 mL
Ground coriander	¼ tsp.	1 mL
Ground cumin	¼ tsp.	1 mL
Salt	¼ tsp.	1 mL
Pepper	⅛ tsp.	0.5 mL
Tofu wieners, cut into thick matchsticks	6	6

Heat cooking oil in frying pan. Add onion and green pepper. Sauté until soft. Remove from heat.

Cook potato in boiling water until just tender when pierced with tip of paring knife. Drain. Add to onion mixture.

Wrap tortillas in foil. Heat in 350°F (175°C) oven for 8 to 10 minutes until warmed but still soft.

Add next 8 ingredients to onion mixture. Heat slowly, stirring gently once or twice, until hot. Add wieners. Heat through. Turn out onto warmed platter. Spoon down center of tortillas. Makes 6.

1 fajita: 261 Calories; 3.2 g Total Fat; 621 mg Sodium; 17 g Protein; 42 g Carbohydrate; 2 g Dietary Fiber

CHICKEN FAJITAS

Preparation time is 25 minutes. A fun meal to eat with your hands. Serve sour cream, lettuce and tomato as condiments.

Condensed chicken broth	¼ **cup**	**60 mL**
Lime juice	¼ **cup**	**60 mL**
Garlic cloves, crushed	**2**	**2**
Dried crushed chilies	½ **tsp.**	**2 mL**
Chili powder	½ **tsp.**	**2 mL**
Ground cumin (optional)	⅛ **tsp.**	**0.5 mL**
Boneless, skinless chicken breast halves	**3**	**3**
Large onion, thinly sliced into rings	**1**	**1**
Green pepper, thinly sliced	**1**	**1**
Red pepper, thinly sliced	**1**	**1**
Flour tortillas (9 inch, 22 cm, size)	**6**	**6**

Combine first 6 ingredients in medium bowl.

Add chicken. Turn to coat. Marinate while preparing vegetables. Heat lightly greased large non-stick frying pan until hot. Remove chicken from marinade. Reserve marinade. Sear chicken in frying pan until browned.

Add onion, peppers and reserved marinade. Toss together. Cover. Cook for 7 minutes until vegetables are tender and chicken is cooked. Remove chicken to cutting board. Slice thinly.

Wrap tortillas in foil. Heat in 350°F (175°C) oven for 8 to 10 minutes until warmed but still soft. Place about ⅔ cup (150 mL) chicken and vegetables down center of each tortilla. Fold up bottom. Fold both sides over center. Makes 6.

1 fajita: 252 Calories; 1.8 g Total Fat; 318 mg Sodium; 20 g Protein; 38 g Carbohydrate; 1 g Dietary Fiber

measurement tables

*T*hroughout this book measurements are given in Conventional and Metric measure. To compensate for differences between the two measurements due to rounding, a full metric measure is not always used. The cup used is the standard 8 fluid ounce. Temperature is given in degrees Fahrenheit and Celsius. Baking pan measurements are in inches and centimetres as well as quarts and litres. An exact metric conversion is given below as well as the working equivalent (Standard Measure).

OVEN TEMPERATURES

Fahrenheit (°F)	Celsius (°C)
175°	80°
200°	95°
225°	110°
250°	120°
275°	140°
300°	150°
325°	160°
350°	175°
375°	190°
400°	205°
425°	220°
450°	230°
475°	240°
500°	260°

SPOONS

Conventional Measure	Metric Exact Conversion Millilitre (mL)	Metric Standard Measure Millilitre (mL)
$1/8$ teaspoon (tsp.)	0.6 mL	0.5 mL
$1/4$ teaspoon (tsp.)	1.2 mL	1 mL
$1/2$ teaspoon (tsp.)	2.4 mL	2 mL
1 teaspoon (tsp.)	4.7 mL	5 mL
2 teaspoons (tsp.)	9.4 mL	10 mL
1 tablespoon (tbsp.)	14.2 mL	15 mL

CUPS

Conventional Measure	Metric Exact Conversion Millilitre (mL)	Metric Standard Measure Millilitre (mL)
$1/4$ cup (4 tbsp.)	56.8 mL	60 mL
$1/3$ cup ($5^{1}/_3$ tbsp.)	75.6 mL	75 mL
$1/2$ cup (8 tbsp.)	113.7 mL	125 mL
$2/3$ cup ($10^{2}/_3$ tbsp.)	151.2 mL	150 mL
$3/4$ cup (12 tbsp.)	170.5 mL	175 mL
1 cup (16 tbsp.)	227.3 mL	250 mL
$4^{1}/_2$ cups	1022.9 mL	1000 mL (1 L)

PANS

Conventional Inches	Metric Centimetres
8x8 inch	20x20 cm
9x9 inch	22x22 cm
9x13 inch	22x33 cm
10x15 inch	25x38 cm
11x17 inch	28x43 cm
8x2 inch round	20x5 cm
9x2 inch round	22x5 cm
10x4$1/2$ inch tube	25x11 cm
8x4x3 inch loaf	20x10x7.5 cm
9x5x3 inch loaf	22x12.5x7.5 cm

DRY MEASUREMENTS

Conventional Measure Ounces (oz.)	Metric Exact Conversion Grams (g)	Metric Standard Measure Grams (g)
1 oz.	28.3 g	28 g
2 oz.	56.7 g	57 g
3 oz.	85.0 g	85 g
4 oz.	113.4 g	125 g
5 oz.	141.7 g	140 g
6 oz.	170.1 g	170 g
7 oz.	198.4 g	200 g
8 oz.	226.8 g	250 g
16 oz.	453.6 g	500 g
32 oz.	907.2 g	1000 g (1 kg)

CASSEROLES (CANADA & BRITAIN)

Standard Size Casserole	Exact Metric Measure
1 qt. (5 cups)	1.13 L
$1^{1}/_2$ qts. ($7^{1}/_2$ cups)	1.69 L
2 qts. (10 cups)	2.25 L
$2^{1}/_2$ qts. ($12^{1}/_2$ cups)	2.81 L
3 qts. (15 cups)	3.38 L
4 qts. (20 cups)	4.5 L
5 qts. (25 cups)	5.63 L

CASSEROLES (UNITED STATES)

Standard Size Casserole	Exact Metric Measure
1 qt. (4 cups)	900 mL
$1^{1}/_2$ qts. (6 cups)	1.35 L
2 qts. (8 cups)	1.8 L
$2^{1}/_2$ qts. (10 cups)	2.25 L
3 qts. (12 cups)	2.7 L
4 qts. (16 cups)	3.6 L
5 qts. (20 cups)	4.5 L

index